"Jaye Martin and Terri Stovall have rendered a valuable service to the Church of the Lord Jesus. *Women Leading Women* is delightful, insightful, and practical. Even more important, it is faithful to the Word of God. Churches and individuals, colleges and seminaries will be guided and helped by this excellent work."

Daniel L. Akin, president, Southeastern Baptist Theological Seminary

"Whether you are a long-term veteran of women's ministry or a novice wondering exactly where to begin, *Women Leading Women* is a must-read for you. Expect to glean valuable wisdom from these two seasoned professionals who carefully lay the biblical foundation for women's ministry then build upon it using the insights learned by their hands-on, personal experiences in ministry. This book is foundational, inspirational, and exceedingly practical."

Marge Lenow, director of Women's Ministry, Bellevue Baptist Church, Memphis, Tennessee

"Enlightening. Inspiring. Readable and practical. Jaye Martin and Terri Stovall have given us a much needed tool for ministry to women in the local church. This book will be used in seminaries, colleges, and churches to teach women the importance of women leading women. It's an invaluable resource. I highly recommend it."

Mary Kassian, Distinguished Professor, The Southern Baptist Theological Seminary

"If there has ever been a time for people in the church to be mentored, it is now. Jaye Martin and Terri Stovall are attempting to help the church in a great way by giving us the biblical model for women from God's Word: women reaching women, and then choosing to mentor them until they are fully engaged, in the context of God's family, being used by Him to reproduce themselves, even as the person who reached them had someone who cared enough to invest. This book will bless the entire ministry of your church. Read it and be blessed!"

Johnny Hunt, pastor, First Baptist Church, Woodstock, Georgia

Between them Jaye Martin and Terri Stovall have decades of experience in women's ministry. Their lives exemplify God's plan for women to reach women through evangelism and discipleship. Their book on leadership provides those of us who are called to minister to women with an invaluable resource. This volume is filled with biblical principles, church-based paradigms, leadership strategies, and personal reflections. It approaches leadership from several perspectives. Based on foundational truths of God's Word it honestly confronts the challenges of our culture while equipping leaders of today and tomorrow to minister to women God's way. I highly recommend this relevant resource and plan to use it as a primary textbook for my classes on leadership for women. I will also recommend it personally to women's ministry leaders in local churches. Women's ministry leaders will benefit immensely from the wisdom of this work!

Rhonda H. Kelley, PhD, adjunct professor of Women's Ministry, New Orleans Baptist Theological Seminary

WOMEN LEADING WOMEN

The Biblical Model for the Church

JAYE MARTIN
& TERRI STOVALL

ACADEMIC
NASHVILLE, TENNESSEE

978-1-4336-9055-6

Published by B&H Publishing Group
Nashville, Tennessee

Dewey Decimal Classification: 248.843
Subject Heading: CHURCH WORK WITH WOMEN \ WOMEN
IN CHURCH WORK \ LEADERSHIP

This trade paper version replaces the original hardcover version
(978-0-8054-4760-6), which is now out of print.

Printed in the United States of America
2 3 4 5 6 7 8 • 20 19 18 17 16

From Jaye:

To Dana

My shepherd, my supporter

To Kelli

My precious angel

From Terri:

To Jay

My protector, my provider
My love

To all those who have mentored and
encouraged us to become the women
we are today

Table of Contents

Foreword   *ix*

Randy Stinson,
*President,
The Council of Biblical Manhood
and Womanhood*

Introduction   *xi*

PART ONE:
BIBLICAL FOUNDATION: WHY WOMEN LEADING WOMEN?

1. Women Through the Eyes of God   *3*
   Terri Stovall

2. God's Plan for Women   *15*
   Terri Stovall

3. The Biblical Paradigm   *29*
   Terri Stovall

PART TWO:
PRINCIPLES FOR WOMEN LEADING WOMEN: WHO WILL LEAD?

4. Following the Leader   *49*
   Jaye Martin

5. Leading like a Godly Woman   *62*
   Jaye Martin

6. Serving with Men   *77*
   Jaye Martin

PART THREE:
THE TASKS OF WOMEN'S MINISTRY: WHAT DO WE DO?

7. REACH Women for Christ   96
   Jaye Martin

8. NURTURE Women in Their Faith   116
   Terri Stovall

9. INVOLVE Women in Kingdom Service   131
   Terri Stovall

10. ENGAGE the Next Generation   142
    Jaye Martin

11. SUPPORT the Church Family   157
    Jaye Martin

PART FOUR:
WOMEN'S MINISTRY IN PRAXIS: HOW DO WE DO IT?

12. Strategic Planning   173
    Terri Stovall

13. Enlisting Your Team   188
    Jaye Martin

14. Living Through Change and Conflict   206
    Jaye Martin

15. Women's Ministry with Excellence   224
    Terri Stovall

Suggested Resources and Bibliography   236
Scripture Index   239
Consulting and Instructional Information   242

Foreword

Who in the world would want to join in the volatile, personal, sensitive, and always colorful gender debate? Why risk being misunderstood? Why put your neck on the line to be accused of chauvinism, feminism, ignorance, or worse?

Well, Jaye Martin and Terri Stovall have jumped in with both feet, and I am glad they did. They are both clear complementarians who care about the home and the church. Both have extensive ministry experience and care deeply about women leading women. And both love the Word of God and want to see more and more women conform to it as they fulfill a Titus 2 ministry in the local church.

My role with the Council on Biblical Manhood and Womanhood over the last eight years has taught me the difficulty of defending the complex biblical and theological nuances of the gender debate, while at the same time trying to express clear points of application for men and women in the home and church. Over the years I have been most criticized when I have tried to detail matters of application based on what I believe are the parameters of the complementarian position. Someone always disagrees. Yet if we do not continue to make these attempts, the gender debate will end up merely being fodder for discussions in seminary cafeterias.

What one believes about gender will naturally dictate the practice of ministry in myriads of situations. So we must continue to attempt to articulate positively the practical outworking of our understanding that men and women are equal in the image of God but different in role and function according to the good plan of God.

This is why I am happy to commend this book—by women, for women—as a step in the right direction for complementarian women asking questions about what it looks like for them to serve in the local church. The authors understand that while there are clear parameters for ministry based on gender, there are hundreds of ministry opportunities for women to teach and lead other women in a Titus 2 fashion.

Thank you, Jaye and Terri, for sticking your necks out, opening yourselves to much criticism, and helping Christian women take some steps in understanding and embracing the high call of leading other women.

Randy Stinson
President, The Council of Biblical Manhood & Womanhood
Dean, School of Leadership and Church Ministry
The Southern Baptist Theological Seminary

Introduction

From Jaye

It is such an honor to introduce you to *Women Leading Women*. It has been years in the making. For more than 20 years I have served in full-time ministry to and with women. They have learned from me, and I have learned from them, and I love them all. I love the ones who served with me into the wee hours of the morning setting tables, and I love the ones who drove me insane with all the things they wanted me to do for them. I love the ones who had a passion for Christ and His Word, and I love the ones who don't even know Him. I love serving with women for the cause of Christ.

Out of this love for women and our Lord, I write this work. God has a plan for women. He desires for us to have the finest and the best that He has to offer. I write because I am concerned that in so many ways the world has wormed its way into our churches and into our ministries. I want us to get back to the basics of what I know that God has called us to do.

God has called us to lead women. I want women to serve the Lord by knowing what the Bible says and how to lead like a godly woman. I want women to know how to serve with men.

God knows that women can reach women like no one else can. He knows that women can nurture and disciple women in such a way that they will get it. He knows that women can minister to women like no man could. God knows that women can train girls to be godly young women. He knows that women can support the church in caring and incredible ways. God knows that women can lead women and that they can do it through the local church. Let's get back to what God's intention was in the beginning. Let's get back to women leading women to the saving grace of Jesus Christ. There is no better way.

From Terri

I have a saying (some students call it my mantra) that I use in every course I teach: you have to know what you believe and why you believe it. I have been reminded in recent days of the battle that we are fighting to uphold biblical truth in the world. In the midst of writing this text, I have stood before media defending the family, the Titus 2 model, and a Proverbs 31 woman. I have listened to more than one former student tell me that she did not realize how much the world (and the church) would challenge her beliefs about women. I have lived a painful family crisis and watched how those with and without Christ have struggled. I have talked to pastors who did not know what to do with their women, and I have had women's ministry leaders cry on my shoulder, trying to figure out how to do "it."

I have also seen the work of God in the lives of women. I had the opportunity to share Christ with a secular media reporter who had never heard the gospel and allowed her to ask the tough questions. I have been able to pray with and talk to family members as never before. I have been able to challenge students to stand firm on what they know to be true, even if they are the only one. I have been able to encourage pastors to hold their women's ministries accountable and have assured struggling women's leaders that God can use them in His kingdom.

We do not live in days when we can fake it. The world will challenge us at every corner, and we are to be ready to stand firm on truth. There are women who need to know Christ, believers who need to grow in their faith, and still others who are dying to find a place of service and connection. My prayer is that we do not allow ourselves to be driven off course from God's original plan for His church and His daughters. I hope that you will embrace the freedom that comes by living a life that reflects a God culture bringing light to a dark world. It is not an easy road to walk, but oh, is it worth it!

Our Passion

We have a passion for the Lord, a passion for the local church, and a passion for women. The truth is, we love to see the three come together the way they were intended. Throw out what you might have seen and heard about women and the church, and let's look at what God's intention was from the beginning. What does God say about the church? What does God say about women? Through years of study for both of us, we have found that God has a passion for the church and a passion for women. He loves the church, and He loves us.

While God loves the church and loves women, sometimes things get mixed up when we try to sort it all out. We have seen churches that don't allow women to do anything and churches that allow women to do everything. We have seen churches with a biblically based ministry to women and churches who do not allow a ministry to women in any shape or form. We have seen women's ministries that are so far from being under the leadership of the church that it is downright scary. We have seen churches allow their ministries to women to have no direction, and we have seen women with attitudes with which any Christian would be disappointed. Frankly, we have seen what God intended for good to be taken to such extremes that it can be hard to find any difference between these ministries and the community charity leagues. These are the things that have compelled us to write.

This is not another book that tells you how to do women's ministry. In the pages that follow, you are not going to find the 10 steps to a successful Bible study or organizational charts for your leadership team. Many good resources are available that focus on the nuts and bolts of women's ministry. The purpose of *Women Leading Women* is to paint a picture of what women's ministry should look like based upon Scripture. We wholeheartedly believe and are operating from the assumption that actions flow out of what one truly believes.

Who will help us get back on track with what real ministry to women needs to look like? Who will equip herself, study the Word of God, and passionately teach what God says? Who will stand up for what is right and lead like a godly, Spirit-filled woman? Who will reach women, teach them, and send them out to do ministry? Who will tell the next generation, and who will do all this under the authority of the local church? Who will help women know that God loves them, sent Jesus to die on the cross for them, and has a plan for their lives? Who will help women know that the local church *is* the plan of God for ministry? Who will stand up and teach what needs to be taught and change what needs to be changed?

We pray that it is you. We pray that you will agree with us that it is time to lead like godly women. It is time to be proud to be a woman who leads other women to the saving grace of Jesus Christ. We pray that you will join us in our charge to bring the ministry to women back under the leadership of the church. We pray that you will join us to make a difference in our homes, in our churches, and in the lives of women and girls.

Women Leading Women: The Biblical Model for the Church is for the kingdom. It is a work that flows out of our passion for the Lord, our passion for the local church, and our passion for women. We pray that together we can make a kingdom difference and that we can make it with women and under the authority of the local church. Jesus died for each of us, but Christ also died for the church. He loves us both. Let's get together.

Now to Him who is able to do above and beyond all that
we ask or think—according to the power that works in
you—to Him be glory in the church and in Christ Jesus to
all generations, forever and ever. Amen (Eph 3:20–21).

Jaye Martin and Terri Stovall

Part One:
The Biblical Foundation
Why Women Leading Women?

*For the time will come when they will not tolerate sound
doctrine, but according to their own desires, will accumulate
teachers for themselves because they have an itch to hear
something new. They will turn away from hearing the
truth and will turn aside to myths. But as for you, keep a
clear head about everything, endure hardship, do the work
of an evangelist, fulfill your ministry (2 Tim 4:3–5).*

We live in a changing world with diverse cultures and a constant exchange of ideals, belief systems, and worldviews. The church today has not remained immune to these changes, and the attacks on biblical truth are constant, many succumbing to the whims of the world, an experiential hermeneutic, and a feel-good theology. Additionally, the rise in evangelical feminism has begun to affect the sight, sound, and taste of the church. Women are leading where women should not lead, men are left sitting on the sidelines (if they are even there at all), and pastors are struggling to figure it all out. It is time to make a stand for the sufficiency of Scripture and God's plan that it teaches for men and women and for the way they serve in the church.

This first section will begin with a look at women as God sees them, women who are created in His image and can be used by Him to make a difference in this world. Having understood who we are in Christ, the second chapter will examine what we are to do and how we are to do it. God has given specific plans and guidelines for women best to be used by Him. Last, we will present the biblical paradigm for a women's ministry in the local church.

The biblical foundation lays the groundwork for the remainder of the text. It is our map and compass for the who, the what, and the how. God's Word is inerrant, infallible, constant, and sufficient. If we are to be true servants and leaders in God's work, then it is time to return to the biblical model for the church.

Chapter 1

Women Through the Eyes of God

Terri Stovall

So God created man in His own image; He created him
in the image of God; He created them male and female. . . . God
saw all that He had made, and it was very good. Evening
came, and then morning: the sixth day (Gen 1:27,31).

We were just closing our women's Bible study for the evening when it happened. She asked *the* question. We were studying the difficult story of Tamar that night. It is a heart-wrenching story of a woman who lost two husbands, was banished to return home to her parents, and finally prostituted herself with her father-in-law in order to become pregnant and bear a child. The women in the Bible study group were uncomfortable with Tamar's story as well as many of the experiences of women in the Old Testament. Like the proverbial elephant in the room, a question was hanging thickly in the air. Julie took a deep breath and asked what each woman in the room was thinking that night. "Why are women treated so badly and have it so hard if God loves us so much?"

I knew that this was not just a question about accounts of lives lived centuries ago. In this room were women who had experienced heartache, hard roads, and pain that ran deep. Many had lived lives parallel to those we were studying and were asking the question, "Do I matter to God?" It is so easy to begin to view ourselves and those around us through the lenses of the world. We seek validation, credibility, and value from those in our lives and the people we encounter. The difficulty with these lenses is that they are flawed and scratched by a sinful and fallen world. Rather than looking through the eyes of the world, we must see women and ourselves through the eyes of God.

Women are highly valued and loved by God. He has used women to impact the lives of families, communities, and the church. This chapter will visit the lives of women in the Old Testament, women in the life of Christ, and women in the New Testament church. Through the stories, challenges, and faithfulness of these women, we will see why God looked down on His newly created woman and said, "It is very good."

WOMEN IN THE OLD TESTAMENT

The Old Testament paints a clear picture of women through God's eyes. From the creation story where God Himself reached down and formed woman in His image, to women leaders who were used by Him for His purpose, to women who remained faithful to God through everyday life, the Old Testament is where the journey begins.

In the movie classic *The Sound of Music,* Julie Andrews' character finds herself struggling to teach her young charges how to sing for the first time. That is when she stops and sings, "Let's start at the very beginning, a very good place to start." When trying to understand and fully grasp the meaning of something, going back to the very beginning often sets the foundation and helps to provide clarity.

Let's go back to the very beginning, when God first breathed the words that brought this world into existence.

GOD CREATED WOMAN IN HIS IMAGE

When God created man and woman, He created them both in His image. Yes, He created man first (Gen 2:7), but that does not diminish the value of woman. He created woman as a part of His original plan, not as a way to say, "Hmm, something's missing." God specifically created man and woman in His image (Gen 1:27) and established the ontological equality of the two. Man was formed out of the dust, and God breathed life into him. Woman was created from man and thus from the same flesh, blood, and breath (Gen 2:22). This ontological equality, or equality in essence, should dispel any idea that one gender is superior to the other. Society today is so performance driven and focused on what a person does, that the being is often lost or dismissed.

God made both man and woman in His image. Man and woman are equal in who and what they are. God was personally involved in forming both man and woman. The focus should not be on who was created first; the focus should be on the fact that God said, "Let us make man in Our image, according to Our likeness," and He did. As women understand that they are created in the image of God and according to His likeness, they can revel in the fact that God looks at each of us and says, "It is very good."

GOD GAVE WOMAN A UNIQUE ROLE

What a woman does flows directly from who she is. She is created from the man and for the man. After God created Adam, God had Adam search for a suitable helper that would complement Adam anthropologically in likeness and his role as leader. Adam needed an *'ezer kenegdo*, a helper that was comparable to him. Adam searched through all the animals and beasts, but found nothing suitable. It was at this point that God formed woman to be his *'ezer kenegdo* (Gen 2:18–20). Man and woman are each given roles and jobs to do that flow directly from who they are. Both fulfill their divine purposes when they live as the people they were created to be and doing what they were created to do—Adam as the spiritual leader and woman as a helper to the man, together glorifying God and revealing God to the world.

GOD USED WOMEN TO LEAD THROUGH THEIR FAITHFULNESS

True leadership is not necessarily something that one seeks but is often a natural outcome of day-to-day faithfulness. There are many examples of women who were used by God out of their faithfulness. Miriam saved her brother, Moses, by being a faithful and attentive sister (Exod 2:1–10). Later she led one of the greatest times of worship for women when she recognized the faithfulness of the one true living God and that poured out on the women around her (Exod 15:20–21).

Huldah was a working woman, the keeper of the royal wardrobe. When Hilkiah found the book of the law and was trying to understand it, he sought out Huldah (2 Kgs 22:14; 2 Chr 34:22). Scripture is not clear about why the king went to her, but if she were not known and respected for her work, her faithfulness, and her walk with God, it is doubtful that she would have been his first choice.

Deborah, a wise woman who was faithful to serve her country and people as a respected judge and "mother to Israel," found herself playing a significant role in battle. This leader of Israel was a strategist and an encourager. She was integral to the success of overtaking King Jabin by encouraging and challenging Barak, who was often insecure. When Barak placed so much hope for victory on Deborah's presence, she was quick to focus his priority on having God with him. Scripture leaves echoes of her faithfulness in the strains of her song proclaiming the works of God (Judg 4–5).

God used Esther, a young Hebrew girl, to save a people from annihilation. An orphan who found herself catching the king's eye, she only knew to do what she was taught to do. She was gracious yet confident, submitting to the authority of the king and her uncle. Esther accepted the fact that God had placed her in a position for just such a time when she could make a difference. Had she not been the courageous, creative, and willing woman that she was created to be, who was faithful to live how she was taught to live, her story could have had a different ending. Instead, God used her, one woman, to save a generation of people.

GOD USED IMPERFECT WOMEN TO CARRY OUT HIS PLAN

One only has to look at the women in the genealogy of Christ to recognize that God did not use perfect women to carry out His plan of redemption. Rather, God used women who, at the end of the day, recognized Him as the one true living God.

The first chapter of Matthew traces the genealogy of Christ, including five women, four of whom are found in the Old Testament. Three of the women (Tamar, Rahab, and Bathsheba) were involved in sexual sin, and two (Rahab and Ruth) were not even Jewish. Tamar, whose story was referenced at the beginning of this chapter, may have taken matters into her own hands. And yes, she was mistreated and wronged. While two wrongs do not make a right, God, in His grace, mercy, and omnipotence, did not allow the sinful actions of mankind to detour His plan. The seed of Israel continued through Tamar (Gen 38).

Rahab, a known prostitute and businesswoman, recognized men of God when she saw them. She risked everything in responding to the God of Israel. Rahab put feet to her faith by trusting that if she followed the instructions of these men of God, she would be saved (Josh 2; 6). Rahab was the mother of Boaz, and the seed of Israel continued.

Ruth, a Moabite woman, while not involved in sexual sin as were Tamar and Rahab, still had her share of pain and heartache. A young woman, widowed and far from home, she remained faithful to the family she had joined and listened to the wisdom of her older mother-in-law. God blessed her with a kinsman-redeemer when she married Boaz. Once again the thread of redemption continues to flow through the life of a woman who walked a difficult path but remained faithful.

7

Bathsheba's familiar story of adultery, murder, and the subsequent death of the son of David and Bathsheba speaks to the fact that all sin results in consequences. While the culture of that day may have made it extremely difficult for Bathsheba to refuse David's advances, it does not excuse Bathsheba's involvement in the tryst. However, Bathsheba and David's story speaks to God's forgiveness and reconciliation when, after a time of contrition, Bathsheba once again bore a son, who was named Solomon (2 Sam 11–12); and the house of David with the seed of the coming Messiah continued.

The women mentioned above are but a small sample of the women whose stories we read in the Old Testament. There are just as many examples of women who struggled, were mistreated, and may not have been considered leaders, but they were faithful. Each of these women recognized that because she was made in the image of God, God loved her, and she was so much more than what man or society might do to her. Although the culture of the day resulted in women being treated in an inferior, sometimes abusive way at times, this does not mean that those who did so were obeying the commands of Scripture. Neither does it mean that women have become damaged or unusable to God. Women are made in the image of God, they are deeply loved and used by God, and no one can change those facts.

WOMEN IN THE LIFE OF CHRIST

Jesus' public ministry on this earth occurred in a culture that was not always kind to women and placed women in a class below men. Many women were considered property to be traded. Jesus, however, made a drastic contrast in the way He treated women versus the way women were generally treated by the culture. From the Gospel accounts, Jesus' attitude toward women was startlingly new for that day. Some may claim that He was countercultural or revolutionary, and truly He was. However, a better description may be that Jesus was reintroducing and modeling God's culture to a world that had been drifting from God's plan since the time of the fall in the garden of Eden. As Christian leaders in the twenty-first century, we too will be seen as countercultural if we consistently live according to God's culture rather than the world's culture. Much is to be learned from Jesus and how He treated women.

JESUS RECOGNIZED THE VALUE OF WOMEN AS PERSONS

The fact that Jesus saw women as individuals and persons rather than objects to be owned was somewhat of a foreign idea to the culture of that time. Women were often viewed as merely sexual beings. Jesus, on the other hand, saw sex and gender as a part of but by no means the whole of a woman. He countered this as He addressed divorce (Matt 10:1–10), used the term "daughter of Abraham" (Luke 13:16), and made it possible for women to accompany Him and His disciples freely without the typical assumptions that they were there for less than moral reasons. Because women were individuals, Jesus held women accountable for their actions and emphasized that each woman had to make her own decision to follow Him. During a day when the head of the house determined the faith of the rest of the family, Jesus confronted women individually and challenged them to make their own faith decision.

JESUS REACHED WOMEN AS WELL AS MEN

At some time in their lives, women, like men, are sinners without a Savior who need to find forgiveness. Like that of men, their sin needs to be dealt with and is never overlooked. Each woman is responsible for her own sin and needs that sin to be forgiven. Consider the adulterous woman. Those who brought her to Jesus were challenged, but her sin was by no means condoned (John 8:1–12).[1] The Samaritan woman was confronted about her sin, and she found forgiveness and a savior (John 4:1–26). When approached by women, Jesus listened to them, held them accountable, healed them, and forgave them. Jesus came, died on the cross, and rose again for both men and women. He intentionally reached out to women during His time on earth.

---

[1] Some manuscripts omit John 7:53–8:11.

Jesus Taught Women

Jesus had a number of significant, intentional conversations with women. He did not approach women as persons of inferior intellect but spoke to women expecting them to learn and understand. He did not address Jewish women only, as two of the longest recorded conversations that Jesus had with women were not Jewish. The Samaritan woman (John 4) and the Syrophoenician woman (Mark 7:26) did not have the religious background or foundation that provided some understanding of who the Messiah was and His message of redemption. Yet He spoke to them expecting them to learn and understand. In the account of Mary and Martha, we find Mary sitting at the feet of Jesus, learning from Him (Luke 10:38–42). Even in His parables He often used subject matters that were familiar to women. He spoke of cooking, cleaning, weddings, childbearing, and widowhood. Jesus taught women and nurtured them in their faith.

Jesus Involved Women in His Ministry

Several times in the Gospels, women are referenced as having been with Jesus, following Him and ministering to Him (Matt 27:55; Mark 15:40–41; Luke 8:1–3). While no specific instances or accounts are given, the clear inference is that women were followers of Christ and actively involved in His ministry. Mary and Martha held a special place in Jesus' life, and it was their home that Jesus used to find rest and nourishment. The testimony of the Samaritan woman led many to faith in Christ (John 4:1–42) . Clearly, women were involved in ministry with Jesus and to Jesus.

Jesus Recognized and Welcomed the Worshipful Service of Women

Jesus honored the widow, who sacrificially gave to God what some saw to be a pittance (Mark 12:42–43; Luke 21:2–3). When Jesus was in Bethany, at the house of Simon, a woman fell at the feet of Jesus, worshipping Him with fragrant oil and tears. Jesus honored her worship and rebuked those who sought to question her actions. Her worship of the Master allowed her to find forgiveness (Matt 26:7; Mark 14:3; Luke 7:37). A woman who served faithfully in the temple was rewarded with a glimpse of the newborn Messiah (Luke 2:36). Women, offering a final act of worship on earth by caring for the body of Jesus, were given a message to proclaim: "He has been raised from the dead" (Matt 18:5–7).

In a day where it was politically correct to treat women as lesser beings, even to the point that it would make a man unclean to touch a woman at certain times, Jesus treated women as God intended from the beginning of time. He would look women in the eyes, looking past the cultural stigma of objects to be owned, and see each woman as a person who needed to know the Messiah.

WOMEN IN THE DEVELOPMENT OF THE NEW TESTAMENT CHURCH

Jesus completed His work on earth and left behind a group of men and women to carry on His gospel message of salvation. Both men and women were active in the development of the New Testament church and were used by the Holy Spirit to spread the good news of Jesus Christ and establish the first communities of believers.

WOMEN PRAYED

After the resurrection the disciples and many others, including women, gathered together in an upper room and united together in prayer (Acts 1:13–14). Paul found himself in Philippi on the Sabbath and went to a place that he knew to be a place of prayer. A group of women was present there, and He began to visit with them, not thinking it unusual that women had gathered to pray (Acts 16:13). Women were actively involved in the development of the New Testament church by joining in the prayers of God's people, as evidenced by Paul's instructions to the church regarding public worship. He instructs a woman to cover her head when she prays

(1 Cor 11:2–16). There is an assumption that women are going to pray in the church.

WOMEN WERE AMONG THE FIRST CONVERTS

Many believers were added, both men and women, in those days following the coming of the Holy Spirit (Acts 5:14). Women were among the first followers of Christ in Samaria (Acts 8:12). In Thessalonica and Berea, Paul and Silas were able to lead many of the prominent Greek women to Christ (Acts 17:4,12).

WOMEN WERE PERSECUTED FOR THEIR FAITH

The persecution of the church included both men and women. Saul went from house to house to find men and women who were Christ's followers and put them in jail (Acts 8:3; 9:2; 22:4). Priscilla "risked her neck" with her husband, Aquila, for Paul (Rom 16:3). No doubt many unnamed heroes and defenders of the faith were women.

WOMEN SERVED IN THE CHURCH

Paul, who regularly thanked those who faithfully served, mentioned the names of many women throughout his epistles. In the sixteenth chapter of Romans alone, Paul greeted or thanked many women, both named and unnamed, who served with him. Included in the list is Phoebe, whom Paul especially spotlights as a significant servant in verses 1 and 2.

In several places Paul mentions Priscilla, who, along with her husband, served faithfully mentoring young ministers of the gospel (Rom 16:3; 2 Tim 4:19; 1 Cor 16:9). Many other women are merely mentioned by name or relationship, but the fact that they were even mentioned signals the importance they had to the spread of the gospel. God equips His children, men and women, to serve Him.

WOMEN WERE INFLUENTIAL IN THE CHURCH

Influence can cause something to happen, be it positive or negative, with seemingly little effort. Paul recognized the influence of women and held women accountable when that influence was counterproductive. Paul recognized the influence of Lois and Eunice on the life of young Timothy (2 Tim 1:3–5). Chloe, in the church at Corinth, was a trusted woman of the faith and one whom Paul sought out in order to discover what was really going on in the church (1 Cor 1:10–11). On the other hand, Euodia and Syntyche were so influential in the church that their personal dispute with each other was threatening the unity of the church, and Paul encouraged the church to help them work it out (Phil 4:2–3). Women could unite or divide, and Paul painstakingly addressed women in his epistles, praising the faithfulness of women and holding women accountable for their negative impact upon the work of the church.

ANSWERING THE QUESTION

Julie's question at the beginning of this chapter is one that is asked by many women every day. Women who are seeking to live as women of God struggle when their experiences seem incongruous to the message of God. The answer to this dilemma is not to look at experiences but to go back to what God says and who He is. Regardless of how women are treated, they are made in the image of God, are used in leadership from the most unexpected places, and play a critical role in carrying out God's plan of redemption. Regardless of the culture, we must follow Jesus by reaching women for Christ, teaching women, allowing women to be a part of His ministry, and recognizing the value and personhood of women. Regardless of gender, every believer has a place of service in God's kingdom and His church. We live in a world and time that promote an experiential hermeneutic that defines truth through our individual, subjective lenses. It is time to remind women and ourselves that experience does not define truth, but God's truth defines our experiences and our lives. The bottom line is that women must not view themselves through the world's eyes but through God's eyes.

QUESTIONS FOR DISCUSSION

1. If you are in Julie's Bible study, how do you answer her question?
2. With which of the women from the Old Testament do you most identify and why? The New Testament?
3. Are there other women from the Bible who were not mentioned in this chapter who can teach us about God's view of women? Who are they, and what can we learn?

Chapter 2

God's Plan for Women

Terri Stovall

But as for you, speak the things which are proper for sound
doctrine: that the older men be sober, reverent, temperate, sound
in faith, in love, in patience; the older women likewise, that they
be reverent in behavior, not slanderers, not given to much wine,
teachers of good things—that they admonish the young women
to love their husbands, to love their children, to be discreet,
chaste, homemakers, good, obedient to their own husbands, that
the word of God may not be blasphemed (Titus 2:1–5 NKJV).

A recent study was conducted examining the influence school playground designs have on the outdoor play of grade school children. One of the elements that researchers examined was the effect of a playground that was bordered by a fence compared with a playground that was not fenced. Researchers discovered that when a playground is fenced, the children will utilize the entire playground for play. It was not unusual to find boys running and playing to the far reaches of the fence line or to find groups of girls huddled together against the fence sharing secrets, laughing, and playing. Conversely, researchers found that when playgrounds were not fenced, the children played closer to the school buildings and rarely, if ever, ventured to the playground boundaries, even if they were told where the edges were.[1] There is safety and freedom in clearly defined boundaries.

Just as a fenced playground gives clear boundaries, allowing the children to run free within its limits, so too does God give women a fence line. Boundaries are not tools to oppress or confine, but first and foremost they allow us to run free safely. This chapter will present the various views of women in ministry, the roles God has given men and women, and the mandate for a woman-to-woman ministry. God has lovingly placed a fence for us that we may find safety, fulfillment, and freedom.

TWO VIEWS OF WOMEN IN MINISTRY

One of the many topics with which Christian women, especially women in ministry, struggle is the concept of submission and male headship in the church and family. Many of the women whom I have the privilege of mentoring desire to be obedient and pure women of God who do not stray beyond God's plan for them. Yet, they struggle to identify exactly where that fence line is placed. The issue of women's roles is one of the issues that can have a tremendous impact on ministries and families in the modern era.

There are two predominant views of women's roles: egalitarian and complementarian. The egalitarian view is the view most readily espoused by evangelical feminists contrasted with the complementarian view held by those whom some have labeled as traditionalists.[2] Let us examine these two views side by side.[3]

---

[1] M. Armitage, "The Influence of School Architecture and Design on the Outdoor Play Experience Within the Primary School," *Paedagogica Historica* 41 (August 2005): 535–53.

[2] The term *traditionalist* has been used by authors such as Linda Belleville in *Two Views on Women in Ministry,* ed. James R. Beck and Craig L. Blomberg (Grand Rapids: Zondervan, 2005), and Alvera Mickelsen in *Women in Ministry: Four Views,* ed. Bonnidell and Robert G.Clouse (Downers Grove, IL: InterVarsity, 1989).

[3] For a deeper study than is possible in this chapter, consult the following sources from which much of this material was gleaned: A. Strauch, *Men and Women: Equal Yet Different* (Littleton: Louis and Roth Publishers, 1999); R. Hove, *Equality in*

MALE-FEMALE EQUALITY

EGALITARIAN	COMPLEMENTARIAN
Men and women are created equal and have equal roles.	Men and women are both created in God's image and have equal standing before the throne of God, but God has given men and women different roles to fulfill.

Egalitarians and complementarians agree that both man and woman are created in the image of God and are therefore created equal. Man and woman relate equally to God. The divide between the two views begins to occur with regard to the roles that men and women are assigned.

ROLES OF MEN AND WOMEN

EGALITARIAN	COMPLEMENTARIAN
Because man and woman are created equal, there are no role distinctions.	Man and woman are equal in being but have different, God-ordained roles to fill.
Role distinctions are the result of the original fall into sin and the subsequent curse. Therefore, redemption in Christ removes role distinctions.	The fall into sin and the subsequent curse did not institute roles. Rather, creation order established the roles and the fall into sin created the struggle to fulfill those roles.
Role distinctions are legalistic and contrary to Scripture and to God.	Role distinctions are freeing not binding. They are given by God to help the man and the woman function together.

For both egalitarians and complementarians the tragedy starts in the garden of Eden with the fall into sin and the curse. While man and woman relate equally to God by nature, complementarians view

---

Christ (Wheaton: Crossway Books, 1999); D. K. Patterson and R. H. Kelley, eds., *Women's Evangelical Commentary: New Testament* (Nashville: B&H Publishing Group, 2006); B. Clouse and R. G. Clouse, eds., *Women in Ministry: Four Views* (Downer's Grove, IL: InterVarsity Press, 1989); J. R. Beck and C. L. Blomberg, eds., *Two Views on Women in Ministry* (Grand Rapids: Zondervan, 2001); and J. Piper and W. Grudem, eds., *Recovering Biblical Manhood and Womanhood: A Response to Evangelical Feminism* (Wheaton: Crossway Books, 2001).

the roles of man and woman as God's way to bring some sense of order in the way man and woman relate to each other. Egalitarians hold that these role distinctions are man-made and are used more to oppress women than to free women. Both views gravitate to two pivotal points: the terms translated "helper who is like" when woman was created, and the curse pronounced upon the woman following the fall into original sin.

A Helper. "Then the Lord God said, "It is not good for the man to be alone. I will make a helper who is like him" (Gen 2:18). The Hebrew phrase that is translated "helper who is like him" or better "helper who is comparable to him," *'ezer kenegdo*, clearly communicates both function and equality. A helper (function) who is like him (created in the image of God) is the creation order established by God. Eve was created in the image of God to be a helper for Adam. Consider the larger picture and the context of woman's creation. God had just paraded every living beast before Adam, and yet Adam was alone because there was nothing like him. Then God created woman, and the minute Adam saw her, he recognized her as one who was like him. Unlike the other beasts that he had named, Adam gave this new creature standing before him a name that echoed his own, for she was part of him. "She shall be called Woman, because she was taken out of Man" (Gen 2:23 NKJV). Adam became leader, protector, and loving guide. Eve provided help and nurture to Adam. "The hallmark of the first male-female relationship was one of unity and equality expressed through complementary, distinctive roles. The created role relationship was one of delightful perfection."[4] Role distinctions were a part of the original creation plan. They did not give value to man and woman's being but brought functional order to man and woman's relationship, enabling man and woman to relate properly to one another.

The Curse. "He said to the woman: I will intensify your labor pains; you will bear children in anguish. Your desire will be for your husband, yet he will dominate you" (Gen 3:16).

---

[4] M. Kassian, *Women, Creation and the Fall* (Westchester: Crossway Books, 1990), 20.

Egalitarians claim that the fall into original sin and the subsequent curse are what established different roles for man and woman, while complementarians say that the curse only explains the struggle that women experience in fulfilling the roles God has designed. Woman's curse was twofold. The first is that she will experience increased pain during childbirth. The implications of this curse is well understood by every woman who has ever given birth to a child. The experience of childbirth is not a curse; rather it is the pain and suffering that go along with it. However, the second part of the curse draws the focus of the current discussion. Some would say that the "desire" a woman has for her husband is a sexual or physical desire. To hold this interpretive view actually yields no curse at all but a gift that God gives man and woman through union in marriage. A better interpretation defines the desire as a desire relating to the role of leader assigned to the man, suggesting that he, in his sinfulness, will dominate or rule over the woman. Whether the woman is trying to usurp the authority of the man or the man is dominating the woman, neither is God's original plan but flows out of a sinful nature. "The best interpretation of the desire-rule clause is that after the Fall, women would rebel against their designated role and that men would abuse their role of leadership, thus creating tension in the male-female relationship."[5]

The curse is more than a judgment but is also an explanation of the relationship of the man and the woman after the fall. Childbirth is not a curse, but sin has distorted God's plan with the introduction of pain and suffering. The role of a man being over a woman is part of God's plan, yet sin causes man to distort that view by becoming domineering. Likewise, desire for a husband is not a curse, but desire for his position and role is the distortion of desire. We do not know what it is like to live in a sinless world, but in our walk of faith to become more Christlike, we should strive to return to living within the roles that God established in His creation order when

---

[5] Ibid., 27.

He first formed man and woman in His image—when this newly formed world was untouched by the destructive nature of sin.

The creation passages are the starting point. Both viewpoints agree that the fall into sin changed the relationship between man and woman. In order to represent correctly the creation order established by God in the beginning, both equality in being and differences in function should be declared.[6] Man and woman are equal in being but have different roles to fulfill. Although functionally subordinate to her husband, the woman's interrelatedness with the man should prevent both from abusing their positions. This creation order is to be the standard for our relationships in the home and in the church.

A WOMAN'S ROLE IN THE CHURCH: WHAT DOES SCRIPTURE SAY?

Egalitarians and complementarians differ on their view of the roles of men and women. This difference is most clearly seen in the role of women in the church. A number of key texts in Scripture have been used to polarize the two views. Space does not allow for an adequate discussion of all of the pertinent passages and interpretations, but let's consider several passages that are regularly presented.

Neither Male nor Female: Galatians 3:28. Written within the context of an extended passage on salvation, Paul writes, "There is neither Jew nor Greek, there is neither slave nor free, there is neither male nor female; for you are all one in Christ Jesus" (Gal 3:28 NKJV). For some this verse erases all role distinctions and opens the door for women to participate in every form of ministry. When dealing with boundaries for women from the pen of Paul elsewhere, evangelical feminists want to make this verse the benchmark so that all other texts are to be understood in relation to this verse. Egalitarians believe that this verse applies both to the relationship with God and to the relationship among men and women.

---

[6] Strauch, *Men and Women*, 7, 25.

In order to understand this verse properly, one must understand its context and the fact that it falls within the framework of salvation. Complementarians correctly recognize Galatians 3:28 is a text within a passage and context discussing salvation by faith in Christ and points to the equality of all in coming to Christ. Paul was writing to a group of people who had been told that the only way truly to be considered Christ's followers was to become like the Jews, specifically that the men had to be circumcised. One of the primary messages Paul was expressing was that Christ died on the cross for all. Standing before the cross there is no Jew, no Greek, no slave, no free, no male, and no female. This has no reference to the roles women fill in the church and in relationship to men. The letter to the church in Galatia, and this focal passage specifically reflects unity in Christ rather than unqualified equality.[7] All are in need of a Savior, and all have a role to fill.

Women's Conduct in the Church: 1 Timothy 2:8–11 and 1 Corinthians 14:33b–38. Several times in his letters, Paul addresses and gives instruction for church worship. Two passages that are often discussed by both egalitarians and complementarians are 1 Timothy 2:11 and 1 Corinthians 14:34. Both passages refer to women either learning in silence or remaining silent in church. Complementarians consider the context to be the public church worship experience and interpret "silence" not to mean absolute silence but a quietness or quiet submissiveness that is respectful of the teaching. Egalitarians believe that Paul was addressing specific situations in specific churches, and thus the injunction does not apply to today. The danger in this hermeneutical approach, however, affects one's view of Scripture. If one holds Scripture high as the inerrant, infallible Word of God and says that a part of God's Word does not count for today, that person is treading upon dangerous ground.

Women Teaching in the Church: 1 Timothy 2:12–15. Paul writes, "And I do not permit a woman to teach or to have authority over man" (v. 12 NKJV). Complementarians believe that this refers to a consistent practice of teaching men the Scriptures. This would

---

[7] Hove, *Equality in Christ,* 105–7.

not preclude the occasional situation when a woman might teach men. But it is the consistent, week-by-week teaching that occurs. A regular teacher naturally possesses some authority over her students; therefore regular teaching and authority go hand in hand. Here again, this refers to the church setting, but in the same way a woman is not to take the lead in the family, she is not to take the lead in the church family.[8] Egalitarians will often dismiss this passage as Paul addressing a specific situation, and thus it is not applicable today. Some will point to the fact that Paul says, "I do not permit" versus "God" or "Jesus" does not permit. Egalitarians will interpret the use of "I" as being Paul's opinion, not the word of God, and therefore dismissive. Here again, this is a dangerous road to travel and still be able to maintain a high view of Scripture.

Because of these and other passages, egalitarians and complementarians differ on the roles that women play in the church. Because they see role differentiation as a result of sin, egalitarians seek to erase all role distinctions by generally saying that women may hold any position within the church, including senior pastor. In denominations that have a hierarchical structure, egalitarians will expand the opportunities to those denominational leaders such as bishop. Complementarians will generally say that women may not hold the position of pastor in the church or other pastoral position where the woman has primary authority over men. These are generalizations as there are differences even among the two views. For example, all complementarians believe that women should not hold the office of pastor in the church. However, there is some disagreement among complementarians whether women should serve in other pastoral positions (e.g., minister of education, single adult minister, student minister, etc.) in the church. The titles used for positions in churches today have muddied the waters, making it difficult to make broad statements regarding specific positions. In general, complementarians believe that women should not have spiritual authority over men in the church on an ongoing basis. Egalitarians say women can do anything in the church; there are no limitations.

---

[8] Strauch, *Men and Women*, 76–77.

Living God's Plan: What to Do

The two views of women's roles, especially in the church, influence women and the church today. How is a woman to know whether she is inside or outside the boundaries given in Scripture? What are the true boundaries that God has placed? This comes back to the mantra I mentioned in the introduction of this text. You have to know what you believe and why you believe it, based upon Scripture. When I was young and new to ministry, I struggled with these issues more than I like to admit. I studied, read, and asked God to show me His ideal. Through the years, as I have seen the results of women stepping outside of the role God has designed, I have become convinced more than ever that true freedom is found living within the boundaries God has set. It is not easy. I am a strong-willed woman. But I place that will under the lordship of Jesus Christ and am developing into a woman who willfully places herself under the authority of others on a daily basis.

One of the specific struggles women face is whether there are certain positions that are appropriate and others that are not. Some have tried to devise lists of positions that are permissible and those that are not, but this distinctive can be difficult to discern in the midst of the many ministries offered by churches today. The best way to know is to seek the Lord and His guidance continually, and He will let you know when you are stepping outside the fence and when you are right where you need to be. Immerse yourself in Scripture, wrestle with and stand under it. Some are reading this and are thinking, *Just give me an example or a picture of what might be inappropriate for women.* One guideline that has worked well for me is that if it looks like Sunday morning then it should be men in leadership rather than women. If it is your primary time that the church comes together, the men are to take the lead.

Another guideline is that if it does not feel right, then it probably isn't, and it is better to err on the side of caution. Hear me clearly. I am not saying to base decisions, theology, or ecclesiology upon feeling. Rather, there are times when God gives us a feeling or a sense that something is not quite right. Use this as a yield sign to stop, look, and listen. Stop what you are doing, look at Scripture, and listen to the voice of God. Sometimes we do not experience these inklings until we are in the middle of it, but that becomes a time to learn that we were a little too close to the line. I experienced that when I was asked by a pastor to come to his church and conduct a training session with the women's leadership team. A few days before my scheduled day there the pastor asked if I would stay for the evening service and share with the congregation what I saw to be the biblical role of women and women's ministry in the church. It wasn't until the service had started that I realized that I was the only person that was going to be speaking that night. They went through their normal music portion of the service, collected the offering, had the special music, and then I was introduced. I knew immediately that I was close to stepping outside of what I believed to be God's boundaries. I was uncomfortable with the setting. At the close of my time, the pastor gave a short conclusion and offered an invitation. God used the invitation time to heal some anger and bitterness between the women's ministry leader and several of the leaders within the church. Some will say, "See, God used you so it must have been okay." I walked away from that night agreeing with God that I would not speak in a main worship service again unless I knew for certain that the pastor would follow me with some biblical teaching. Trust the feelings and intuitions God gives you. Just because God moved and worked does not automatically put a stamp of approval on our role in the process. We don't base everything on feelings, but they should be signals to stop, look, and listen.

I can already hear the "ifs," "whens," and "buts." If I had to categorize the concerns or struggles that women have, they would be these three. First, "I will submit to my husband if he loves me as Christ loves the church." Or, "I will submit to the authority of the pastor except when he doesn't do what I think he should do." I call this the *Eve complex.* That is, it's my husband's fault when I am not submissive. The only problem with this is that God did not include the word *if* in writing His Word. God simply says, "Wives, submit yourselves to your husbands as unto the Lord." Our behavior is not dependent upon the behavior of our husbands. I have yet to meet a wife who does not desire her husband to be the leader of the home. As you submit to your husband, God can do a powerful work in the life of your husband and the family. Likewise, as women submit to the authority of their pastors, opportunities for ministry and influence will present themselves like never before. It is not your job to make sure that those who are in authority over you do their part right. Your responsibility is to ensure that you are living and acting in the way God has commanded and designed.

Second, "I will let the men lead when a man steps up to the plate." I call this the *fill the gap complex*. If there is a need, we as women are very quick to meet that need. Scripture is not conditional when it speaks on male leadership in the church. It does not say, "If there are no men available, then women should lead the church." As women, there are times that we need just to sit, wait, and leave the leadership gaps so that God will have the opportunity to raise up men to step into leadership. This allows us to step into the places of ministry designed for us, not for someone else.

Last, "But I have been given the gift of speaking and preaching. I must be called to be a pastor." This is the *nothing but pastor complex*. You very well may have a gift and talent for opening Scripture, explaining the Word, and being able to communicate truth effectively. The church needs women who can rightly handle the Word of God and effectively communicate His truths to women. God is creative and He gifted you. Ask Him what He has planned for you.

Amazing freedom and protection are afforded to women when they willfully place themselves under the authority of the leaders in their lives. You should search the Scriptures, search your own heart, and determine what you believe to be the role of women in ministry. I shared that I am strong-willed woman, as I know many of you are. When you submit your strong will to the Lord, to your church leaders, and to your husband, you place yourself in the best possible position to impact this world for Christ. It may not make sense funneled through the world's paradigm, a paradigm of ifs, whens, and buts. God's paradigm, on the other hand, says, "Just follow what I have commanded and trust Me." Graciously submitting to the roles that God has created for you to fill is not God's oppression; it is His gift of freedom.

WOMAN-TO-WOMAN MINISTRY

Traveling through a town in Algeria, I was sitting on a bus watching the women as we drove by. The women walking those streets will never hear the gospel of Jesus Christ unless a woman tells them. In the church today, teenage girls are growing up without godly mothers to teach them how to be a wife and mother God's way. Women are searching for spirituality and need women who will teach them the truth from God's Word. God has given women the command to make disciples just as He has given men the same command. The best way for women to fulfill that command is through woman-to-woman ministry.

Paul's letter to Titus gives the best outline for what pure women's ministry is to be. The passage referenced in the title of this chapter tells us who is to be involved, what is to be done, and what we should expect from it. The older women are to take the lead in woman-to-woman ministry. While the term *older* can mean biologically older, it can also be understood as spiritually more mature. Expectations are placed on this mature woman. The qualifications listed by Paul reflect a woman of high regard. She is respectful, possesses good judgment, is not pulled into gossip sessions or acts of misjudgment. She is a teacher of good things. It is impossible truly to teach that which one does not know; therefore she knows and lives what she teaches. The younger women are the focus of woman-to-woman ministry. Just as *older* can mean senior in years or spiritually mature in the faith, *younger* can mean younger in years or new and fresh to the faith. Woman-to-woman ministry is bringing the older and the younger together to teach and to learn. It is the older woman reaching and nurturing the younger woman.

Paul also offers what is to be taught, the curriculum, if you will. Woman-to-woman ministry is to teach women to love their husbands and to love their children. As wives, we love our husbands differently than as mothers we love our children, but both are equally important. One cannot be sacrificed for the other. Woman-to-woman ministry is to teach women to be discreet and chaste. Women are to be taught how to be sensible and pure, especially sexually pure. We live in a day when the sexual purity of women is challenged on a daily basis. Women can teach women how to live lives of purity in the face of a world where impurity is celebrated. Woman-to-woman ministry is also to teach women to be homemakers, good women, and women who are submissive to their husbands. Note that all of these relate to the home and help to guard the sanctity of the home.

The result of woman-to-woman ministry is "that the word of God may not be blasphemed." How can teaching women all these things keep the Word of God from being blasphemed? Such teaching reinforces the roles that God created from the moment He established His creation order and spoke this world into being. It reinforces the instructions from God's Word for what it means to be a follower of Christ and a woman after God's heart. It teaches a woman to be the woman, wife, and mother God has created her to be. Woman-to-woman ministry provides one of the best ways for women to make disciples by reaching and teaching other women.

WHAT WOMEN DO

Many women today hear that they cannot do anything in the church. On the contrary, there is much for women to do and to be done. We have a world full of women who need to know the redemptive message of Jesus Christ and how to receive the gift of life. These same women need to know how to grow in their faith and become fully developing followers of Christ. Too many times, women get caught in the trap of wanting what they should not have. They long for that one piece that we have been told not to touch. (Sounds a lot like Eve doesn't it?) In the meantime an entire garden of opportunities goes unnoticed.

What can women do in the church? They can do anything they have been gifted and called to do within the boundaries and guidelines that God has placed. What we as women do flows out of who we are. We have been created in the image of God and have been given a role to fulfill. We serve a loving creative God who is using women to impact the world for Him in a thousand different ways. Enjoy the freedom of living under the authority and grace of almighty God. It is as if God has given us a fenced playground and there is a lot of room to play.

QUESTIONS FOR DISCUSSION

1. If you were asked about your view of women in ministry, how would you answer the question and support it biblically?
2. From a study of Scripture, what are the benefits of men and women living within the roles that God created from the beginning?
3. How can the curriculum in Titus 2 be taught in women's ministry today?

Chapter 3

The Biblical Paradigm

Terri Stovall

*And let us be concerned about one another in order to promote
love and good works, not staying away from our meetings,
as some habitually do, but encouraging each other, and all
the more as you see the day drawing near (Heb 10:24–25).*

R ecently a group of women gathered to celebrate the work
that God had done in their lives. These women were
accomplished authors, influential speakers, and key leaders within the Christian community. What began as a time that I
looked forward to attending quickly became an opportunity for God
to sound warning bells and wave red flags in my heart and soul.
Many of the attitudes and images portrayed seemed more secular
than Christian and illustrated a number of the complaints I have
heard from pastors who were frustrated with women leaders. The
most disturbing thing that occurred at this event, however, was not
even presented by a woman.

A noted researcher in the area of church and religious life was
slated as the keynote speaker and the primary reason I was there. I
looked forward to hearing an overview of his soon-to-be-released

book and especially anticipated updates on his latest research as it applied to women. Five minutes into his presentation my heart sank, and I felt myself becoming defensive. The presenter began to outline research that he suggested showed the local church no longer met the spiritual needs of many in the United States and thus concluded that the local church was a plan that had seen its time. He felt that God was now using many other avenues for reaching people for Christ, and if his projections held, over the next twenty-five years the local church would become ineffective, possibly bordering on becoming obsolete. He ended his presentation by asking the audience to withhold judgment until we had read his complete text.

I returned to my hotel room that night and spent many hours in prayer and searching Scripture. My soul was disturbed. What is the role of the church? Is it truly a plan that has seen its better days, or was this presupposition one more way for Satan to move the people of God from His ideal? What about the growth of women's organizations and conferences that are so popular today and are not connected to a local church ministry? The answer to these questions, and to the hypotheses presented that day, is the same as it has been from the beginning of the New Testament church in Acts. God can move through many different avenues and in many venues; however, He has commanded the body of believers to fellowship together and to reach this world for Christ—together. Just because, on the human plane, some local churches have become ineffective, God's plan does not necessarily change. The problem is not with God's plan, but with man's execution of that plan. As God's people assemble themselves together under the authority of Jesus Christ they accomplish God's mission of reconciliation for the world. Likewise, successful, biblical women's leadership and woman-to-woman ministry best operates under the authority of the local church to reach women and families for Christ.

THE MASTER PLAN

God has given the Church His paradigm for leadership. Before delving into the various parts of this paradigm as it specifically relates to women leading women, it is important to stop and look at the big picture. It is not the purpose of this chapter to serve as part of a systematic theology book but rather to affirm and reacquaint ourselves with the theology of the Church.[1] How one carries out a plan or task is affected by that person's core belief system. Likewise, how we carry out the work of the church is affected by our ecclesiology.

The Church can be defined as the community of all true believers for all time,[2] the universal Church. It is a living organism, a body, created for worshipping and glorifying God. One must understand who the Church is created to be before one can understand what she is commanded to do and how to do it. The nature of the Church is the place to start. Whom did God create the Church to be, and what is her essential character? Once the essential character of the Church is understood, then it is time to move on to the mission of the Church.

As God has created and given the body of Christ life, He has also given her a mission. He has not left the Church to wander aimlessly or to struggle with what she is to do. God has very clearly stated His mission in both the Great Commission and the Great Commandments (Matt 22:37–40; 28:18–20). They are the Church's marching orders and define what is to be accomplished.

At this point the focus shifts from the universal Church to the local church body. Each local church has been placed in a certain location at a certain time in order to reach a certain people. A local church must define her specific mission, that is, how she will play her part in fulfilling the universal mission of the Church. The local church's mission is then carried out through the five functions of the church: evangelism, discipleship, worship, ministry, and fellowship.

Within a specific local church body are numerous ministries, each given its own purpose and defined set of methods or functions. This is where successful women's leadership and woman-to-woman

---

[1] For the sake of discussion, it is important to differentiate between the universal Church and the local church body. The universal Church will be indicated by spelling the word *church* with a capital *C* and the local church body will always be designated by spelling the word *church* with a lower case *c*.

[2] W. Grudem, *Systematic Theology: An Introduction to Biblical Doctrine* (Grand Rapids: Zondervan, 1994), 853.

ministry occur. Each ministry area must determine the purpose God has for it and how this area of service will help the local church body accomplish its mission, thus fulfilling God's universal mission for the Church. After a women's ministry identifies its unique purpose within the local church body, then that purpose is accomplished through the five functions of reaching, nurturing, involving, engaging, and supporting. The purpose and functions of women's ministry relate directly to the mission and functions of the local church. The mission and functions of the local church relate to God's universal mission for the Church. The universal mission for the Church flows out of the nature of the Church. All of this is under the umbrella of giving worship, honor, and glory to God (see Diagram 1).

This gives a quick flyover and looks at the big picture of God's paradigm. Let's look at each part of this paradigm in more detail.

THE NATURE OF THE CHURCH

American society is a performance-driven society. Whenever someone says, "Tell me a little about yourself," we often start with what we do. We will speak about the work we do, the position we hold, or the roles we play when introducing ourselves to others. This is not our nature. Nature refers to the essential character that defines who we are. Am I loving, gentle, kind? Am I a person who is driven, or am I more laissez-faire? Am I a person of integrity? Am I consistent, or am I swayed by changing times? It is character through which all action flows. We are ultimately defined not by what we do but by who we are. Likewise, the nature of the church relates to the essential character that defines the body of Christ and through which all actions flow.

A study of Scripture shows many analogies, word pictures, and descriptions that paint a portrait of the Church. From God's Word we learn the Church is a body that has a divine purpose and a reconciling ministry. It is a body that shares and prays. The Church is gifted and called, always working together in unity.[3]

---

[3] M. H. Maynard, *We're Here for the Churches* (Nashville: LifeWay Press, 2001), 10–11.

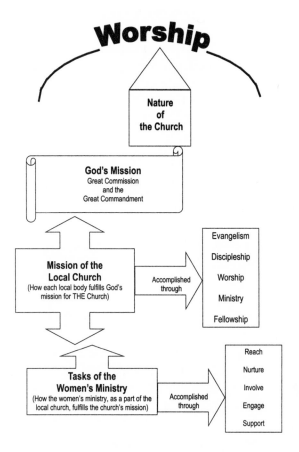

Diagram 1: The Biblical Paradigm

The Church is a body that worships (Eph 1:6,12,14; Rom 11:33–36; 25:9–11; Heb 13:15; 1 Pet 2:9; Acts 16:25–34; Matt 5:16). The Greek word for church in the New Testament, *ekklēsia,* means an assembly or gathering of people. For the Church, the sole purpose of assembling together is to worship the one true living God. It is the basic nature of this assembly to worship and is one of the essential characteristics of the true Church of God. Everything the Church is

33

and everything the Church does fall under the umbrella of worship. It is the primary driving force for its existence.

Christ is the authority. The Church is under the authority of Jesus Christ. Christ established His Church on earth and is the head of the Church. This makes Him both the center of all the Church is and her head and authority (Matt 16:18 and Col 1:18). An organism cannot have more than one head and be healthy, nor can it ever become separated from the head and still live. In today's world medical advances have made it possible for people to live without many body parts. We can live without arms and leg. Heart machines can pump blood for us. Lung machines can breathe for us. Dialysis allows us to live with nonfunctioning kidneys. We can receive transplants for almost every organ in the body, and yet the one thing the body cannot do is live without the head. Life cannot be artificially sustained without a head. Likewise, the Church cannot live without her head, Jesus Christ. If the Church becomes disconnected from the head, even for a moment, she instantly begins to die.

The Holy Spirit empowers the Church. As the Church is connected to the head, Jesus Christ, so the Holy Spirit empowers the Church. A study of the book of Acts and the early expansion of the Church offer a glimpse at the Holy Spirit at work among God's people. Every instance of growth, movement, and addition to the kingdom of God references the work of the Holy Spirit (see Acts 2:4; 8:29; 11:12; 13:4 for a sampling of the many references). As the Church must remain connected to the head, it must also keep the conduit of power open through the Holy Spirit.

God gives the Church a glimpse of her character and nature through many different word pictures. Some of the metaphors that are used to describe the church include branches on a vine (John 15:5), the body of Christ (1 Cor 12:12–17) or the whole body (Eph 1:22–23; 4:15–16; Col 2:19), family member (1 Tim 5:1–2; Eph 3:14; Matt 12:49–50; 1 John 3:14–18), and God's field (1 Cor 3:6–9). This is by no means an exhaustive list but a sampling of the many different metaphors used for the Church in the New Testament. Why is it so important to understand the nature of the Church?

Each of the metaphors and word pictures describing the Church is a way for God to communicate who the Church is created to be. Grudem seems to put it best:

> The fact that the church is like a family should increase our love and fellowship with one another. The thought that the church is like a bride of Christ should stimulate us to strive for greater purity and holiness, and also greater love for Christ and submission to Him. The image of the church as branches in a vine should cause us to rest in him more fully. The idea of an agricultural crop should encourage us to continue growing in the Christian life and obtaining for ourselves and others the proper spiritual nutrients to grow. The picture of the church as God's new temple should increase our awareness of God's very presence dwelling in our midst as we meet. The metaphor of the church as the body of Christ should increase our interdependence on one another and our appreciation for the diversity of gifts within the body.[4]

As the Church understands who she is and revels in the amazing body that God has created, only then can she truly fulfill the mission of God. For any living being, actions flow from the heart and the Church is no exception.

GOD'S MISSION FOR HIS CHURCH

The Church is a body with a divine purpose and mission. The Church exists to represent Christ in the world in order to accomplish His desire to reconcile the world to Himself. His body, the Church, must be a redeeming presence in the world and communicate the reconciling message of the gospel. The Church originated in the mind of God and was created to serve His purposes.

The Great Commission is God's mission. While expressed and reiterated many times throughout the New Testament, many hold

---

[4] Grudem, *Systematic Theology,* 859. See also chapters 44–48 for an in-depth study of the theology of the Church.

the Great Commission as the penultimate statement of God's mission for the Church. It defines what the Church is to do.

> *Then Jesus came near and said to them, "All authority*
> *has been given to Me in heaven and on earth. Go,*
> *therefore, and make disciples of all nations, baptizing*
> *them in the name of the Father and of the Son and of*
> *the Holy Spirit, teaching them to observe everything I*
> *have commanded you. And remember, I am with you*
> *always, to the end of the age" (Matt 28:18–20).*

Discussions of this passage often begin with verse 19, but we must start with verse 18. Jesus said, "All authority is given to me." He does not say that He has given us the authority but that He still possesses the authority to call men to Himself. This reinforces the earlier discussion that it is only as the Church remains connected to the head, Jesus Christ, that she can truly fulfill the mission God has given her.

Through the authority of Jesus Christ, the Church has been given the mission to "go and make disciples." There is both an assumption and a command to go. The Church is not aimlessly wandering but intentionally going with the purpose of making disciples. What methods should be used? The Church is to make disciples by baptizing and teaching. We are to introduce and lead people to faith in Christ and then walk beside them to help them grow in their walk with Christ.

The Great Commandments are the how. They direct the manner in which this mission is to be carried out. Christ is adamant that everything His followers do must stem from love, love for God and love for others.

> *He said to him, "Love the Lord your God with all*
> *your heart, with all your soul, and with all your*
> *mind. This is the greatest and most important*
> *commandment. The second is like it: Love your neighbor*
> *as yourself. All the Law and the Prophets depend*
> *on these two commandments" (Matt 22:37–40).*

Loving with all your heart, soul, and mind is a wholehearted devotion to God and includes the whole body. When Jesus was asked what the greatest commandment is, He quickly went to love. It is as His followers love with their entire beings that they cannot help but follow all His commands.

Jesus does not name a second commandment but has essentially named a tie for first place. As we love the Lord with our whole body, soul, and mind, can we not help but love others? Conversely, if we struggle with loving others, we must question whether we truly love God with all our heart, soul, and mind. As we connect with God and love Him completely, do we not become as Christ and therefore are compelled to love others even as ourselves? If the Church does anything that does not flow from loving God, loving others, and making disciples, is it truly doing what God has created it to be and do? Paul reminds the church at Corinth of this command to love (1 Cor 13) and expresses to Timothy that everything he does has love as its goal.

Now the goal of our instruction is love from a pure heart,
a good conscience, and a sincere faith (1 Tim 1:5).

God has created the Church as a living body that reflects the nature of Christ. He has called the body of Christ to love Him with every ounce of its being. God has commanded His children to love others with the love of Christ and through that love to go and make disciples.

THE MISSION AND FUNCTIONS OF THE LOCAL CHURCH

The previous discussion on the nature and mission of the Church is focused on the universal Church. While the universal Church refers to all true believers for all time, the local church is a community of believers that meets together on a regular basis. There are many types of meeting places for local churches (i.e., homes, coffee shops, schools, theaters, and traditional church buildings). Many different groups, denominations, sects, and cults consider themselves to be a "church." For our purposes, *a local church* will refer to a group of believers in Christ who meet on a regular basis in a particular location, have a structure of organization and authority, rightly teach the gospel, practice baptism and the Lord's Supper (or Communion), and are committed to fulfilling God's mission by joining together to form a local body of believers.

Each local church that is a true church has been placed by God at a particular time, in a particular place, with an ability to reach a particular people. A church in Oxnard, California, is able to reach a particular people to which a church in Tyler, Texas, may not have access. The church in Tyler, Texas, works in a culture that is different from the culture where a church in Minneapolis, Minnesota, exists. The church in Minnesota has opportunities to reach people in 2009 that the same church did not have in 1955. Each local church must determine what role God has ordained for her to play in accomplishing His universal mission for the Church.

The Mission of the Local Church

In both church growth and secular business books today, the importance of a mission statement is heavily stressed. Whether it is called a mission statement, vision statement, or purpose statement, the important point of the exercise is to focus church members (or employees in secular business) on what they are doing and why they are doing it. Identifying the mission God has given the local church becomes the sieve through which all activity is filtered. As the local church verbalizes and reinforces the reason it exists today, every ministry, every action, and every decision should have as its end enabling the church to accomplish her mission.

A local church should ask four questions to identify the specific mission and vision God has. Four questions have been suggested to help the church determine what God has for her.

1. Why does the church exist?
2. What are we to be as a church? (Who and what are we?)

3. What are we to do as a church? (What does God want done in this community and in this world by this body of believers?)
4. How are we to do it?[5]

These simple questions mirror the biblical paradigm. Start with a reason for existing. Then move to understanding who you are created to be. From there, begin to seek what you are to do and how you are to do it. The answers to these questions will be similar but different for each local body of believers. It is evident that each church has the same universal mission; however, the specific method and role that each church plays in accomplishing God's universal mission will look a little different.[6]

THE FUNCTIONS OF THE CHURCH

Where the mission of the church is the *why*, the five functions of the church—evangelism, discipleship, worship, fellowship, and ministry—are the *what*. They are what the church does to accomplish the mission of the church. These five functions are universal for all churches and flow out of a New Testament understanding of what God is calling churches to do. How each local body of believers carries out these functions will look different. For example, all churches have the function of worship, but each church will worship differently. Even within a local church, there can be different ways to carry out the function of worship. Let's look at each of these a little closer.

Evangelism. Evangelism is intentionally proclaiming the truth of the gospel of Jesus Christ in the power and leading of the Holy Spirit. Evangelism is not just telling people what Christ has done for them but includes inviting nonbelievers to repent and accept Christ as Lord and Savior. Too many times we share the gospel but stop short of asking for a response. Evangelism is a proclamation of the life, death, burial, and resurrection of Jesus Christ. This echoes the

---

[5] R. Warren, *The Purpose Driven Church* (Grand Rapids: Zondervan Publishing House, 1995), 98.

[6] An in-depth discussion on identifying God's vision and mission for the church and its ministries will be addressed in chapter 12.

foundational commandment found in the Great Commission to "go and make disciples, baptizing . . ." A call both to an individual effort by each follower of Christ and to the entire church to evangelize, Christ's church represents a redeeming presence in the world. The church is to communicate the reconciling message of the gospel not only to persons nearby but to all persons everywhere.

The local church carries out the function of evangelism through a myriad of methods. Each church service can offer a call to repentance. Special events can be evangelistic in purpose. Intentionally confronting today's culture through community involvement is evangelistic. Mission involvement in North America and around the globe is for the sole purpose of seeing people come to Christ. The key is intentionally presenting the gospel to nonbelievers and then asking for a response to accept the good news of the message of Christ.

Discipleship. Discipleship, the second function, is the obligation of the church to nurture those who are already believers and build them up in maturity in the faith. The work of transformation into the likeness of Christ is the work of God. Part of the process of growing in Christ is learning what it means to be a follower of Christ. This answers the second part of the Great Commandment: "Go and make disciples . . . teaching." In Paul's letter to the Colossians, it is clear that believers are not just to win people to Christ but that "we proclaim Him, warning and teaching everyone with all wisdom, so that we may present everyone mature in Christ" (Col 1:28). The church has the responsibility to teach, exhort, encourage, rebuke, and discipline one another (Col 3:15–16; Heb 10:24–25).

Worship. Worship, the third function, is both a description of the nature of the church and the function of the church. The church's purpose is to worship God, responding to His presence. Worship in the church occurs formally and informally, in large groups and in small. Paul gave instruction regarding the practice of corporate worship in several of his epistles (see Col 3; Eph 5:1; 1 Cor 12–14). Worship is to be both a corporate and an individual experience. The church that carries out the function of worship well provides opportunities for corporate worship but also disciples its members to experience personal worship. Worship activities may include prayer, thanksgiving, singing, testifying, preaching, reading Scripture, proclamation, and giving (Acts 2:42; Eph 5:19; Col 3:16; 1 Cor 16:2; 1 Tim 2:1–2; 4:13).[7]

Ministry. The fourth function is ministry. Ministry is the church meeting human needs in the name of Christ. It is lovingly serving others and meeting their needs as a natural outflow of faith. It models the sacrificial, self-giving love of Jesus. Jesus is clear that this ministry of mercy is both for those inside the church (Acts 11:29; 2 Cor 8:4; 1 John 3:17) and to unbelievers (Luke 6:35–36). The distinction between the church meeting physical needs and secular organizations, such as the Red Cross, is the fact that it is done in His name and for His glory. Ministry means a concern for the spiritual, mental, emotional, and physical well-being for people inside and outside the body of Christ. How this function is carried out is dictated by the people whom God has placed in its ministry sphere. An inner-city church that has been placed close to an area where the homeless congregate will fulfill this function differently than a church located near a children's hospital that can minister to parents of sick children during a difficult experience.

Fellowship. The final function is fellowship. Fellowship is a reflection of the trinitarian God through believers loving one another as God loves us. Many churches have been accused of performing this function so well it seems that it is all they do. There are a time and a place for the church to encourage its members and other followers of Christ to express, nurture, and preserve the oneness they share because they know Christ. Fellowship is the coming together of people with the commonality of experiencing Christ's saving grace under the unity of the Spirit with love, forgiveness, patience, and the common goal of worship and service of God. Through fellowship, unity is cultivated. A study of the "one another" passages in the New Testament offers a snapshot of the multiple expressions of fellowship and mutuality that are to be practiced by the local church

---

[7] Maynard, *We're Here for the Church,* 12.

(John 13:34–35; 1 Cor 12:25; Rom 12:10; Gal 4:3; 5:2; Eph 4:32; 1 Thess 5:11; Heb 10:24; Jas 5:16).

The five functions of the church together make it possible for the church to accomplish the *missio Dei*, the mission of God. Some churches will do certain functions better than others, but every church should be doing all the functions to some degree. Balance is a key. We are to be about reaching people for Christ through evangelism and then discipling them to become fully developing followers of Christ. The church must lead its people into the presence of God to experience true worship. The body of Christ must take care of one another and reach out to meet the physical, emotional, and spiritual needs of those outside the church. We have been called to encourage one another, celebrate together, pray together, hold one another accountable, and break bread together through fellowship. When the local church engages in the five functions of the church to meet the specific purpose God has given that particular community of believers, then the *missio Dei* is fulfilled.

THE PURPOSE AND TASKS OF WOMAN-TO-WOMAN MINISTRY

We have spent a considerable amount of time in this chapter walking through the nature and mission of the Church and the mission and functions of the local church before reaching the place of women's ministry. As was discussed in chapter 2, there is a definite command and order regarding the role of women in the church. Women's ministry and women's leadership best exist under the authority of the local church and its pastor.

Each ministry within the local church has a specific group of people to reach, minister to, and disciple. The children's ministry focuses on children and their families. The youth ministry reaches out to teenagers and their families. The music ministry focuses upon worship opportunities to carry out the functions of the church through music. The women's ministry is about reaching, making disciples, and ministering to women and their families. It is a ministry that is best led by women serving under the authority of a local church.

The Purpose of a Women's Ministry. The women's ministry in a local church should determine how, as a part of the local church, it will help fulfill the church's mission and vision. It too can verbalize and have written a specific purpose statement that communicates to the church why the women's ministry exists. The women's ministry must recognize and verbalize that its purpose must relate directly to the mission and vision of the church, working in concert rather than in competition with it.

The purpose statement of a women's ministry will, like the church's mission statement, be the sieve through which all activities are filtered. With an appropriate understanding of why the women's ministry exists, women leaders can begin to set objectives and goals to accomplish that purpose.

The Tasks of the Women's Ministry. Understanding the purpose of the women's ministry answers the *why* questions. *How* this purpose is fulfilled is through five tasks of the women's ministry. The tasks of a women's ministry are to *reach, involve, nurture, support,* and *engage.* Each task is carried out within a community of believers in fellowship all for and through worship to God. The five tasks of a women's ministry overlap with one another, reflecting a balance of ministry.

The first task is to *reach* women for Christ, and it relates directly to the evangelism function of the church. Reaching women for Christ involves all the actions of the ministry that engage the culture to share the gospel and ask for a response. It asks the question, "What are we doing that is intentionally evangelistic and reaching those women who are not followers of Christ?" The activities in this task go far beyond inviting women to an event at the church. Yes, it is using events, but it is also making sure the events are intentionally evangelistic

43

where the gospel is clearly presented and an opportunity to respond is offered. It is helping women develop a lifestyle of evangelism where they intentionally seek out opportunities outside the church for the purpose of building relationships with unbelievers in order to share what Christ has done for them. It is equipping and educating women on the cultural concerns of today in order to enter into effective dialogue with the community always with the goal of sharing the love of God.

The second task for a women's ministry is *nurture*. A successful women's ministry will nurture women in their faith. This relates directly to the discipleship function of the church. This task asks the question, "What are we doing to help women become fully developing followers of Christ?" The nurture task involves activities such as mentoring, women's Bible studies and accountability groups. A women's ministry that is carrying out the nurturing function well involves women in Bible study that is dynamic, life changing, and significant. It is creating an atmosphere where the Titus 2 standard is reality and true mentoring occurs. Women's ministries that are effectively nurturing women have opportunities for growth for all levels of spiritual maturity from the seeker to the new Christian to the woman who is ready to step into leadership.

Involve is the third task of a successful women's ministry. The question here is, "What are we doing to involve women in meeting the needs of others through ministry and mission opportunities?" One of the foundational activities of this task is helping each woman in the church find her place of service. While this means helping a woman identify her spiritual gifts, talents, and passion, it is so much more. It is working with and walking with the woman until she has found the place of service God has for her. Women's ministries that are successful at this task know how to work with volunteers and are creative in identifying areas of service. It is the principle of "every member a minister" in action.

The fourth task is to *engage* the next generation. This task asks, "What are we doing to make a difference in the lives of today's teenage and college girls?" So much of women's ministry is helping women deal with the consequences of poor decisions or behaviors while teenagers are in college. A successful women's ministry will invest in the lives of these young women to model a Titus 2 ministry at a critical developmental age. Girls today are faced with situations, issues, temptations, and choices as never before. Why not have mature Christian women walking beside them as they traverse this treacherous time? This task will have an impact on lives today and on the family and the church in the future.

The final task for a successful women's ministry is to *support* the work and ministries of the church. This function answers the question, What are we doing to support the local church programs by identifying needs, filling those needs, or partnering with other ministries in the church? The church is a body comprised of many parts, and the women's ministry is just one part. Sometimes the other areas of the church need a helping hand. Other times there is a specific ministry void or need that the women's ministry can fill. In supporting the other ministries of the church, women's ministry can move miles ahead as a valued ministry in the eyes of the church and make the most dramatic impact for God's kingdom. Has the children's area recognized that a large number of unchurched mothers are bringing their children to VBS? The women's ministry can partner with the children's ministry to offer something to these women. Are there a number of single parents in the church who are struggling this Christmas? The women's ministry can do a type of "Angel Tree" for the children of those families. Are the youth taking a mission trip to Mexico? The women's ministry can partner with them and go on the trip for the purpose of reaching out to the Mexican women. There are so many ways that the women's ministry can support and work with the other ministries in the church and together accomplish the mission and vision God has given.

THE PARADIGM REVISITED

A paradigm is defined as a pattern or an example of something. God has given us His paradigm for carrying out His mission. He has set the pattern for how the church should exist, and He has set the boundaries and example of how women should lead. Successful, God-centered women's ministry works under the authority of the local church. The purpose and tasks of the women's ministry relate directly to the mission and functions of the local church. They work in concert and in harmony when the women's ministry follows the lead of the local church, its pastor, and staff.

The local church's mission and functions relate to the *missio Dei* for the church. God has given every church a universal mission found in the Great Commission and the Great Commandments. Yet, because each local church has been placed at a specific location, in a specific culture, at a specific time, how God's mission is accomplished looks different from church to church.

The Great Commission and the Great Commandments communicate God's mission, which flows out of the nature of the church. The Church is the bride of Christ with certain characteristics that reflect its Creator.

Each part of this paradigm must operate where it has been placed. Should the Church try to separate itself from its head, it will die. The local church cannot decide to look for a different mission than the one God has given, or it ceases to be a true church. The women's ministry, as should all ministries of the local church, serves within the authority of the local church to make the greatest impact in the lives of people. Then a women's ministry is truly successful in bringing glory and honor to Jesus Christ.

QUESTIONS FOR DISCUSSION

1. What is the mission statement for your church?
2. What is the purpose statement for the women's ministry in your church?
3. How does your women's ministry help the church accomplish its mission?
4. What are some practical ways that a women's ministry carries out the five tasks: reach, nurture, involve, engage, and support?

Part Two:
Principles for Women Leading Women
Who Will Lead?

My heart is with the leaders of Israel, with the volunteers of the people. Praise the Lord! (Judg 5:9)

here is something innate in a man that wants to rescue a woman and something deep inside a woman that wants a man to rescue her. When a woman is experiencing a hardship in her life, often she needs the counsel of a godly woman. When a pastor or male minister has a woman come to him who needs wise counsel, he needs to entrust her to a godly woman who can lead her and show her wise counsel.

In the perverse postmodern culture in which we find ourselves, pastors must protect themselves—not protect themselves from the women of the church, but protect themselves from the temptation to be drawn in just because they are human men created in the image of God with the passion to protect and to rescue. Every pastor needs his wife (if he is married) and a few godly women to whom he may entrust the women. Titus 2 is clear that the older women are to encourage the younger women. The pastor should have a few women he can trust. We believe that every church needs a woman enlisted to lead. Every pastor needs one or more to whom he can refer to lead the women of the church.

So the questions are: Who will lead the women? What are the leadership qualities that are needed? For what do we look in a woman leader? How do women serve with men? In this section, in chapter 4 we will look first at the character of God for our general principles of leadership that a woman needs to possess. In chapter 5 we will look at some of the specific areas that give women the greatest challenges. In the last chapter in this section, chapter 6, we will deal with the truths of women serving with men and touch on some of the things to know to best communicate and work with men.

This section on the *who* of leadership is for every woman who leads or desires to be a leader God can use. It is also a section that we feel the pastor may be able to benefit from so he will know what to look for as he enlists a woman to serve under him in the ministry to and leadership of women in the local church.

Chapter 4

Following the Leader

Jaye Martin

He has told you men what is good and what it is the LORD
requires of you: Only to act justly, to love faithfulness,
and to walk humbly with your God (Mic 6:8).

Life isn't fair, people are not always faithful, and pride is the
original sin. Maybe that's why Micah tells us that all God
requires of us is to "act justly, to love faithfulness, and to
walk humbly." Don't we wish that every leader would just do that?
Leadership is complicated. Being a leader in ministry can get more
complicated. Being a woman leader in ministry just adds one more
challenge. In order to find out what God intended, we have to go
back to His Word and see what leadership should be about. With so
many books out there on leadership and so many people speaking on
the topic, sometimes we get confused about what leadership should
look like. We run to the latest bestseller and take it all in, sometimes
forgetting that while it may be full of truth, there are some things
mixed in that may not be God's truth. In this chapter we will look
at what leadership is and define it, look at God as the author of
leadership—who He is and what He does—discuss whether leaders

are gifted or called, and end on the importance of following God before attempting to lead.

WHERE ARE THE LEADERS?

Will the real leader please stand up? Where *have* all the leaders gone? It is time to talk honestly about a real problem in this fallen world that we live in. It's time to talk about godly leadership. It's our greatest problem. Maybe you expected me to say that our greatest problem is that families are falling apart, and they are. Maybe you expected me to say that pornography and drugs are at the forefront, and they are. Maybe you thought I would tell you that the people of the world need to be saved, and of course that too is true. We could go on and on with the list of all the things wrong with the world—all the sins, if you will—but the greatest problem that I see is a lack of godly leadership. It is the lack of men and women of God who will step up to the plate and be the godly, faithful, fair, and humble leaders that God calls them to be. It is the lack of men and women who will stand up for what is right and pure and holy and unashamedly fight for God, His plan, and His principles on how to live. The problem is men and women who look the other way when they see wrong—even when they can do something about it. When are we going to figure out that God sent Jesus to show us how to lead and expected us to follow His lead? God sent Jesus to model how to live in such a way that people would see God in Him and that God would be glorified. That's what leadership is all about. It is about sharing the greater vision of Jesus Christ, how to know Him personally, and how to lead others to do the same. Godly leadership is not waiting for someone to ask you to lead; godly leadership is following Christ so closely that you know how to lead and you do it in such a way that you model Christ by your every word and action while influencing others to do the same.

LEADERSHIP IS VISIONARY INFLUENCE

To define *leaders* and *leadership* adequately, we should think about where all of this started. God is the Creator of all things as we clearly see in Genesis 1. He created the first man and woman and gave each responsibilities to carry out (Gen 1:27–31; 2:15–25). He set the boundaries and kept in contact with those He created (Gen 2–4). God is visionary influence. He is the ultimate leader.

LEADERSHIP DEFINED

Let's define *leadership*. In Joseph C. Rost's book, *Leadership for the Twenty-first Century*, he gives "four essential elements of leadership that flow from the definition: (1) a relationship based on influence, (2) leaders and followers develop that relationship, (3) they intend real changes, and (4) they have mutual purposes."[1] I would define it even more simply: leadership is visionary influence. It is leading and modeling how to lead. It is showing others how to follow. The one who leads sees where people need to go and influences people to follow. You will find thousands of books on leadership. At the time of this writing, there were 156,000,000 Web pages that came up in a Google search of the word *leadership*; so there is plenty out there should you want to dive a little deeper into the subject or choose another definition. However, we are going to look at leadership from a biblical perspective. What does the Bible say, and what do women need to know about leadership in general? I am convinced that the reason we have problems in the church is because of people and, specifically, leaders. We have a huge leadership problem in the church. Unfortunately, this huge problem often begins with us. Let's start at the beginning and look at what God's Word says about leadership. The best way to change the world is one person at a time, so let's begin with ourselves.

MANAGEMENT DEFINED

Management can be defined as taking care of things, people, projects, and situations. It is people doing good things but not necessarily casting the vision or creating new things. Managers may manage things and people, but they don't have to have followers. Managers

---

[1] J. C. Rost, *Leadership for the Twenty-first Century* (Westport: Praeger Publishers, 1991), 127.

usually carry out the vision that a leader set. Managers give the how-to on how to accomplish the tasks at hand. Management is not leadership, and leadership is not management. Management takes the relationship out of work. While certainly management comes from God and requires people to be Spirit filled, it is not what we will be dealing with in this chapter. We will focus our attention on being a leader, and being an effective, Spirit-filled one at that.

God: The Original Leader

God is the original, ultimate leader. Good leadership principles come from Him and from who He is. They flow out of His character. When God's leadership principles are followed, people will find success in carrying out His plan in His way. Ultimately, God is in control. He is the source of truth and the foundation for everything. He is the true foundation for leadership. He is the original leader.

The definition of leadership is built on the foundation of the Creator Leader, God Himself. To be an effective leader, one must base her leadership on God. This is a servant style of leadership that balances the characteristics of who He is with what God created that person to be. When we understand who He is, we will then understand the characteristics that are essential for us as leaders.

When I began to do in-depth study on leadership, I had to process through the concept that all leaders come from God. It is easy to take godly leaders who are successful and see how they have depended on God and how He has blessed their leadership. The part that concerned me was that there were numbers of leaders out there who did not know God, did not care to know Him, and certainly rejected any influence of Him in their lives. Yet God is still the author of leadership. And our leadership is at its best when we are filled with His Spirit.

Spirit-Filled Leaders

There are numerous good examples of leaders in the Scriptures. Some may have been more gifted than others, some may have been more obedient, but we can learn from all of them. When I think of leaders in the Bible, several come to mind. Nehemiah, Moses, Deborah, Joseph, Daniel, Paul, and Lydia are just a few. These were great men and women who chose to follow God. They became great leaders because God had gifted them but also because they allowed God to lead them.

Spirit-filled leaders are those who have accepted Christ as their Savior and come before Him on a daily basis, allowing Him to forgive them and cleanse them of wrongdoing. To be Spirit filled is to empty oneself of anything except Christ. It means that we say no to things that are not of God and focus on what God tells us to do. He tells us things through His Word, and nothing He tells us will contradict Scripture. God also uses other people and circumstances to guide us. We constantly seek God and His wisdom to be the Spirit-filled leaders that He longs for us to be. The question for us is, Will we follow and be all He desires us to be?

WHO HE IS—HIS CHARACTER

God is true and honest, holy and pure, right and righteous, just and merciful, compassionate and gracious, wise, hope, peace, love, patient, faithful and forever, and the list goes on. His character is who He is. He is the model for leadership. He shows us how to lead and live through His Son, Jesus Christ. Christ's example on earth is the very picture of what a leader should look like. The Bible is our best text on leadership.

GOD IS TRUE AND HONEST

Jesus told him, "I am the way, the truth, and the life. No one comes to the Father except through Me" (John 14:6).

God is true and honest. That's who He is. There is no lie in Him because that is part of His character. He cannot be true and untrue at the same time. There are no contradictions in Him. Being true means being absolute and consistent. God is true regardless of who believes in Him. We strive to be honest, trustworthy, and truthful in every aspect of our lives. One of the most important things we need to do in this postmodern world is insist on integrity. People need to know that we are living out our beliefs on a daily basis. In every aspect of ministry, we evaluate every action to be sure that we are being truthful and honest in all of our dealings. Because He is true and honest, we must be as well.

GOD IS HOLY AND PURE

And one called to another: Holy, holy, holy is the LORD
of Hosts; His glory fills the whole earth (Isa 6:3).

God is holy and pure. There is no impurity in Him. He cannot look on evil. He is a God without blemish; He is a God who is free from all flaws. As leaders, we can only be holy and pure by coming before Him and allowing Him to cleanse and sanctify us. We do not assume that saying a quick "God forgive me" will do it. We take the time necessary to repent and to allow Him to remove our impurities and make us holy. We are to be holy because He is holy. Only those who have come before Him on a continual basis can be holy and pure leaders. When we disregard our need for Him, we lose our effectiveness to be the holy and pure leaders that He calls us to be.

GOD IS RIGHT AND RIGHTEOUS

The LORD is righteous in all His ways and
gracious in all His acts (Ps 145:17).

God is right and righteous. He is never wrong and always blameless and upright. He is the One who is always virtuous in every way. Leaders strive to represent God in every endeavor. While we are sinful by nature, we can seek God and His rightness in every situation. We can know that He will guide us in being righteous and gracious in every action that we take.

GOD IS JUST AND MERCIFUL

And if you address as Father the One who judges
impartially based on each one's work, you are
to conduct yourselves in reverence during this
time of temporary residence (1 Pet 1:17).

God is a just and fair God. He judges each one's work impartially and makes fair decisions. He sees the whole picture and can be trusted to be merciful in the judging process. As leaders, we just look to Him to help us see the whole picture in every situation. We are to be just and fair in our demeanor. We should be full of mercy and redemption yet still be just and fair.

GOD IS COMPASSIONATE AND GRACIOUS

But You, Lord, are a compassionate
and gracious God, slow to anger and abundant
in faithful love and truth (Ps 86:15).

God is a compassionate and gracious God. He sees the needs and He fills them. He is gracious in His dealings with people. He is considerate and caring. He shows compassion by showing us the way to go in a sensitive, caring way. As women, we are to be caring and considerate as we deal with other people. We are to look to God to give us His compassion in difficult situations. God always sees the eternal and redeeming value in His creations, and we need to see the same. We are to be empathetic and kind as we deal with every person in our lives.

GOD IS WISE

To the only wise God, through Jesus Christ—to
Him be the glory forever! Amen (Rom 16:27).

All wisdom comes from God, who is wise. When we want wisdom, we ask for it. He is the author of wisdom and always knows the right thing to do and say. He is knowledge but more than that,

He knows how to apply it. God longs to grant us wisdom in every situation in which we find ourselves. As leaders, we call on the God of wisdom to show us how to lead in every aspect of leadership. We are wise leaders when we tap into Him.

GOD IS HOPE

Now may the God of hope fill you with all joy and peace in believing, so that you may overflow with hope by the power of the Holy Spirit (Rom 15:13).

Hope is who He is. He is the author of hope. God can fill us with hope and peace as we believe and trust Him in everything and every situation. As He fills us, we overflow with hope by His power that is available through the Holy Spirit. Women need hope. Everyone does. We need leaders who can hope in the promises of God. This is not just a hope that something will happen but the hope of knowing that the promises of God will be fulfilled. It is essential that we pass on the hope of God to those to whom we minister.

GOD IS PEACE

God is not a God of disorder but of peace (1 Cor 14:33).

God is the author of peace. God is peace. He is not the God of disorder. Inner peace is one of the most important things that women can have, and God is the only one who can bring peace in this troubled world we find ourselves. Leaders learn to come to the God of peace and allow Him to transfer His peace to us by the power of the Holy Spirit. Leaders also look to bring peace to troubled people in troubled situations. His peace is one of order, and He is the peace of promise upon whom we can depend.

GOD IS LOVE

Give thanks to the LORD, for He is good; His faithful love endures forever (1 Chr 16:34).

God is love. He is the foundation for unconditional acceptance and understanding. God's love is good and His faithful love endures forever. Most people do not understand unconditional love and what acceptance is all about. In the church we show the love of Christ to each person and at all times. It is easy to say we love people, but it is hard to do it and to show it. People will be able to feel the love of Christ by our words and our actions.

GOD IS PATIENT

The Lord does not delay His promise, as some understand delay, but is patient with you, not wanting any to perish, but all to come to repentance (2 Pet 3:9).

God is the definition of patience. When no one else is enduring and tolerant, He is. When others have had their patience run out, He is still there with staying power. He is patient. People are not always patient. All too often we give up on people. Not only do we give up on them coming to Christ, but we give up in lots of ways. We lose patience with people even in little ways. As women leaders, we learn patience and show patience to all. Even if we are flustered with people, we learn to persist in God's loving patience for them and for the situation.

GOD IS FAITHFUL AND FOREVER

LORD, Your word is forever; it is firmly fixed in heaven. Your faithfulness is for all generations; You established the earth, and it stands firm (Ps 119:89–90).

God is faithful to all people at all times and to all generations. He is faithful forever. People are not faithful. Sometimes people believe that God is not faithful so we show them faithfulness in all we say and do. Faithfulness is about being loyal, true, trustworthy, and consistent. It means being devoted, dedicated, and committed. Being faithful is who God is, and we are able to be faithful because He is faithful. Women need to see that leaders can be faithful servants in all walks of life.

The character of God, who He is, gives us a glimpse of how we are to lead. Scripture is full of how to love God and how to relate to others. These are important truths in the realm of leadership.

WHAT DOES HIS CHARACTER LOOK LIKE IN US?

> *But the fruit of the Spirit is love, joy, peace, patience,*
> *kindness, goodness, faith, gentleness, self-control.*
> *Against such things there is no law (Gal 5:22–23).*

What does God's character look like in us? The result of the Spirit of God in our lives can be seen through the fruit of the Spirit. It seems like such a basic Christian principle, but in fact these traits are the very things that give leaders the most trouble. It is not the big things that get us; it is the little things. Things like not being nice to people, not controlling our anger, being impatient or agitated, forgetting that the one who is standing at our desks, interrupting our ministry, *is* our ministry. It is understood that most of those who are asked to leave staff ministry positions are asked to do so because of people problems. It is sad to think that this is true. We are to be so connected to God that many of our immediate reactions are tempered by the Holy Spirit working in us. When we do blow it, we should be coming back and apologizing to everyone involved. None of us is perfect, and that is the main reason we stay in tune and allow the Spirit of God to work in us, and the result of Him will be seen no matter what the circumstance.

Therefore, God's chosen ones, holy and loved, put on heartfelt compassion, kindness, humility, gentleness, and patience (Col 3:12).

GIFTED OR CALLED?

> *Based on the gift they have received, everyone*
> *should use it to serve others, as good managers*
> *of the varied grace of God (1 Pet 4:10).*

If God gave gifts to men, then we know that God had to be those things to give them. He can give leadership because He is the leader. He can give teaching ability because He is the teacher. He can give people the ability to shepherd because He is the shepherd. The list goes on. God is who He says He is and that is His character. While we could look at many aspects of His character, we will focus on the fact that God is the ultimate leader. We need to be looking to Him and His Word on just how to lead.

There has been discussion for years whether leaders are born or bred. The answer is both are true. Some are gifted by God, but as Christians, we are all called to lead. Leaders are those who see what needs to happen and then know how to make it happen. They know how to follow God and, while doing so, know how to lead others. It is that balance of total submission to Him and His vision but yet total confidence in themselves as leaders. People follow people with vision.

The next question then arises, Does he give everyone the same level of leadership abilities? Another way to ask it would be, "Does God give everyone the same leadership potential?" The gift of leadership is given by God for the purpose of leading in the local church to direct the members of the body of Christ in fulfilling the purpose of the church. It is the ability to hear God's vision, based on the truths of His Word, and lead people to work together to accomplish God's plan.

> *According to the grace given to us, we have different gifts: If prophecy, use it according to the standard of faith; if service, in service; if teaching, in teaching; if exhorting, in exhortation; giving, with generosity; leading, with diligence; showing mercy, with cheerfulness (Rom 12:6–8).*

The gift of administration is given by God for the purpose of managing the entities of the church in accomplishing the plan of God. It is the ability to organize and implement the plans given by God to the leader.

"And God has placed these in the church: first apostles, second prophets, third teachers, next, miracles, then gifts of healing, helping, managing, various kinds of languages" (1 Cor 12:28).

Each of us has, by the very fact that we are believers, the calling and the capacity to lead. Some are gifted in leadership and so that gift is obvious to all. Consider the fact that we are all called to serve, yet some have the gift of service. Many of us are called to teach, but some of us are especially gifted in teaching. We are all called to be encouragers, yet some are have the gift of exhortation. Whether we are gifted in the gift of leadership or not, we are all called to lead. The question is *how* will we lead?

FOLLOW . . . AND LEAD

God shows us who He is through His Word, through His Son, and through the Holy Spirit. As we read through the Scriptures, we see how He revealed Himself to so many. His commandments show us the principles of how to live, but they are all based on who He is. He is the one, true God, who desires to have a relationship with us. He is the God of protection and provision. His laws flow out of who He is. He desires for us to know Him and to follow Him.

Follow-ship becomes the great challenge. We need leaders who will follow *the* Leader. We need leaders who, on a daily basis, will look to Him before they look to make a name for themselves. Whether leadership is given or learned is not the key issue; the key issue is that to be effective leaders, we are to be obedient on a moment-by-moment basis to the leading of the Holy Spirit. We must do what Micah 6:8 reminds us to do: act justly, love faithfulness, and walk humbly with our Lord. Philippians 2:1–11 on the humility of Christ should be our model as leaders. We have to take on the same attitude of Christ and serve fairly and with humility. God is the one who rewards and lifts us up. We lift Him up as we serve faithfully. "Humble yourselves before the Lord, and He will exalt you" (Jas 4:10). "Whoever exalts himself will be humbled, and whoever humbles himself will be exalted" (Matt 23:12).

IN CONCLUSION

To follow Jesus in truth and humility is the ultimate sign of being a leader. Certainly Jesus showed us in every way how to live and how to lead to make a difference in this life. Everyone has the ability to choose whom he or she will follow. "Choose for yourselves today the one you will worship. . . . As for me and my family, we will worship the LORD" (Josh 24:15).

QUESTIONS FOR DISCUSSION

1. Who are some examples of good leaders that you know? What makes each a good leader?
2. Who are the leaders in the Bible? Discuss both the things they did right and the things they did wrong. What can we learn from each of them?
3. Look at each of the attributes of God. How can we live out His character as we lead in ministry?
4. Study the biblical passages on being gifted and being called. What are the differences between these two? How does God call and gift women to serve?

Chapter 5

Leading like a Godly Woman

Jaye Martin

*Do nothing out of rivalry or conceit, but in humility
consider others as more important than yourselves.
Everyone should look out not only for his own interests, but also for the interests of others (Phil 2:3–4).*

I was in junior high when I finally understood that anyone
could lead. It was the first week, and since everyone was at
a new school, the playing field seemed to be equal. I didn't
understand why I was a leader at the first elementary school that
I went to and at my next one I wasn't, but I was determined to
figure it out. That first week in homeroom, I learned a valuable
lesson: we must vote for ourselves. Our teacher announced that
we would have elections for student council. A boy pointed to
another boy to nominate and a girl pointed to me. She wrote our
two names on the board and had everyone vote. The boys voted
for him and the girls voted for me. I voted for him. There were
21 in the room, ten boys and eleven girls. What was I thinking?
From as early as I can remember, I was told to put others first.
Where did it get me? Student Council Alternate. To this very
day, I have relived that decision many times. Where is the line
between being a strong leader who believes in herself and being

supportive and putting others first? It is a daily challenge to learn to lead women while we still follow Him.

Even though there are general leadership principles for every leader, a few are unique to women. In order for women to be godly leaders, it is essential that these skills be developed. In this chapter we will look at the parts of leadership with which women seem to have the most trouble. These are the leadership characteristics that every godly woman leader needs to know.

LEADERSHIP CHARACTERISTICS OF A GODLY WOMAN

FAITHFUL WITH SMALL THINGS

Maybe the hardest lesson that I have had to learn is this one: be faithful with small things. One of my favorite parables is the one about the talents. We find it in Matthew 25:14–30. This is the story of a man who is headed on a journey and entrusts his property to his servants. To one he gives five talents, to another two, and the third just gets one. Since a talent was in fact the money of the day, each handled his allotment in a different way. The one who received five talents put his money to work for him and gained five more. The one with two talents gained two more. However, the man who just got one dug a hole in the ground and hid his master's money. When the master returned, here's what he said to the ones who had doubled his money: "His master said to him, 'Well done, good and faithful slave! You were faithful over a few things; I will put you in charge of many things. Enter your master's joy!'" (Matt 25:21). To the one who had hidden the money, the master took the talent back and gave it to the one who had ten. Then we read, "For to everyone who has, more will be given, and he will have more than enough. But from the one who does not have, even what he has will be taken away from him" (Matt 25:29). Jesus was clear that He would bless those who are faithful with small things.

Whatever God gives us to do—even if we see it as insignificant— we are to do it and do it with excellence. We are to be faithful with the small things, the small jobs that we are given, and God will reward us by giving us more.

As a women's minister on staff at a large church, I saw this principle disregarded so many times. Someone would tell me that she felt like God was calling her to be a big name speaker or singer or the leader of one of our ministries. How thrilling it was to have a volunteer. Yet often the same person wanted to start at the top. Even though she had never held any job in the church, she wanted to walk in and have the same respect as those who had paid the price of leadership for years. For instance, let's say that a woman wanted to teach one of the Bible studies. Let me give you a profile and assure you that it will fit more than a few hundred to whom I have talked. She goes to a Bible study but can't get there every week. She isn't on time because of her busy schedule and can't stay late since she has to pick up the kids. She's been a Christian for 10 years but hasn't ever read the Bible through and isn't into Scripture memory. She doesn't give to the church because she's never gotten in the habit. She's never shared her faith because she doesn't have that "gift." She's never taken on any other responsibilities at church such as greeting, bringing snacks, organizing parties, or the like, but she is ready to teach and she looks at me like I'm the big bad monster who is keeping her from experiencing God's perfect will in her life. Need I go on?

When I was a young adult, God called me out of the interior design world and into the ministry of sharing Christ with others. I was still doing interior design, but God gave me new interiors to work with that had eternal significance. I closed my business and began to follow Him by going to seminary and preparing for ministry. I was the overexcited housewife with whom no one knew what to do.

I was involved in reaching out to youth, and even though I drove the leaders crazy, many of them were glad to have an extra hand around to get things done. I began to realize that I had to be faithful with small things, do anything and everything, and just see what I could learn in the process. Two full years after I finished seminary, I finally got a full-time ministry job. I did everything from fill-in secretarial work (I typed 29 words a minute; the average was probably around 50 or 60) and other temporary work, to organizing files, buying supplies, cleaning up offices, running errands, and other really important things. I learned obedience. I learned to follow directions and do it someone else's way. I learned to be a servant and to see the need and fill it. I learned humility and that I was very replaceable at any minute. I'm glad those days are over, but I want you to know from the bottom of my heart that I could do it again. It doesn't bother me to make my own copies or set up my own room. It is nice when someone else does it, but I can still do it without getting bent out of shape. I learned what it was like to work for someone else, and I learned to be respectful of those who work with me. I learned what not to do as much as what to do. All of it made me a better leader today than I ever would or could have been otherwise. I thank God for the opportunity to serve in small ways.

In those days I camped in Philippians 2:1–18. This passage is often referred to as the hymn of Christ. I used it as a guide to write how I should live my life. Another passage that I spent a lot of time in was Philippians 3:12–14: "Not that I have already reached the goal or am already fully mature, but I make every effort to take hold of it because I also have been taken hold of by Christ Jesus. Brothers, I do not consider myself to have taken hold of it. But one thing I do: forgetting what is behind and reaching forward to what is ahead, I pursue as my goal the prize promised by God's heavenly call in Christ Jesus." God is faithful to us when we are faithful with small things.

Passionate Aim

Passion and purpose are things that only God can give. Effective women leaders are passionate and have a biblical direction to their passion. Think about the women leaders whom you know. Chances are God has given them a passion for something and they are enthusiastic about that purpose to which God has called them. Women follow women with passion and who know where they are going.

We may think we are passionate about that to which God has called us, but when we get out there with a little bump in the road, we can change our priorities in a hurry. If someone questions or gets upset with us, we are off and running, just sure that it was all a mistake and that we must not be on the right pathway.

Passionate aim is something that God stirs deep within us. It is what drives us and motivates us. It makes us get up in the morning and keeps us from going to bed at night. It occupies our time, our energy and all our very being. Passionate aim is who we are in Christ. It is the driving force behind what we do and why we do it. It is who we are when no one else is around. It is what makes us tick. Passionate aim is what people need and want in their lives.

Jesus was passionate. He was passionate about His mission. He was passionate about spending time with the Father on a daily basis. He was passionate about people and making sure they heard the message of truth and love and salvation. He never tired of telling stories. He never tired of healing souls. It drove him in every area and walked Him to the cross. Don't get the idea that He was never tired physically because we know that He was. But He never stopped His mission because a greater force, His heavenly Father, compelled Him.

God gives everyone a passion to fulfill the purpose or calling He has for his or her life. Maybe that calling is in full-time ministry or maybe it is not. Each one is called to know Christ, share Him, and lead others to do the same. However, each one will do it with different gifts and in different ways. Everyone won't be the big name speaker. Everyone won't be Mother Teresa. Women should be passionate about the ministry to which God has called them. Discover the reason you are in this world and make the most of it. If you want to make a difference, you have to find out what your passion is. You have to learn who you are and what gifts and talents you have and what God's plan is for your life.

How do we do that? As we sit down with the Father, He begins to unfold His plan for our lives. What an incredible picture we see in Jeremiah 29:11–13, "'For I know the plans I have for you'—[this is]

the Lord's declaration—'plans for [your] welfare, not for disaster, to give you a future and a hope. You will call to Me and come and pray to Me, and I will listen to you. You will seek Me and find Me when you search for Me with all your heart." God wants us to come to Him and seek Him. The best part is He lets us find Him. He desires to give us His passion and purpose for our lives.

Many make the mistake of thinking that their passion comes from within themselves. Passion can come from anywhere but the passion that changes lives is the passion that comes from God. He does not count on us mustering up something ourselves; in fact, I am quite sure that He plans on being the sole supplier of our passion. When it comes from Him and we spend time with Him, then He can grow and develop the passion that He has placed within us.

COURAGEOUS RISK TAKING

If we long to make a difference in the life we have on this earth, then we must be willing to be courageous and take risks. God gave Joshua a great lesson in Joshua 1:3–9. The Israelites were preparing to cross the Jordan into the promised land. God told them in verses 3–5 that He would give them every place where they set their feet. He would extend their territory, and no one would be able to stand up against them all the days of their lives. He promised to be with them and never to leave or forsake them. God told Joshua three times to be strong and courageous. God also told Joshua how to do this. In verses 3–6, God showed that He was faithful. In verses 7–8, the command was given to meditate on His Word, and in verse 9, the reminder is there that God would always be with them. The only way to be strong and courageous is to depend on God's faithfulness, stay in the Word, and remember that He will walk with us every step or leap of the way. Courage is something we have to pursue. We can't just sit and wait for courage to come to us; we must go after it.

The other part of being courageous is that of taking risks. We must be willing to take risks but must also know when to take them. When we look at the concept of risk, timing is very important. I cannot help but think of the times that I rushed into one of my boss's offices with a passion to talk (or sometimes raise my voice) about a particular issue. I thank God that the times when I was in passionate pursuit of a matter and about to risk my job that the one I was there to see was not there or had someone in his office. When God was in something and I was totally prayed up and calm, I could walk in and all the doors would be open and the timing perfect. Those of us willing to risk must watch the timing so we do not ruin a good thing.

In developing a national ministry to women in the area of evangelism, timing is very important. Lots of prayer must go into planning before things take place. Most of us want everything now. We must learn to be strategic and get with God about His plan and His timing. When we are in the Word on a daily basis, we will be sensitive to Him, and He will help us know when the timing is right.

INTEGRITY

Jesus said, "Blessed are the pure in heart, because they will see God" (Matt 5:8). We are to be clean in heart. There should be no impurity in us. We should be free from a mixture of what is false or not genuine, blameless and innocent and unstained. I can hear the passion in Paul's voice when he tells of his prayer in Philippians 1:9–11:

> *And I pray this: that your love will keep on growing*
> *in knowledge and every kind of discernment, so*
> *that you can determine what really matters and can*
> *be pure and blameless in the day of Christ, filled*
> *with the fruit of righteousness that comes through*
> *Jesus Christ, to the glory and praise of God."*

As we apply Paul's prayer to our lives, his prayer for us would be that our love would grow, that we would be in the Word and with the Father, so that we would be able to know what is pure. He would also want us to be filled with the result of righteous living in order that God be praised and glorified to the extent that everyone else could see it in order to make a kingdom difference. This was the purity of which Jesus spoke. It is the purity that allows us to see God and allows others to see God in us.

Another way to look at purity is via integrity. Integrity is something that comes from the inside and reaches to the outside. Integrity is the essence of purity. Integrity is when beliefs, morals, and ethics are integrated and are one. It is our character and who we really are. Anything we do that does not line up with what we say we believe causes us to lack integrity. Without purity and integrity others will not be able to understand the message of Christ in today's world.

Consistency is one aspect of integrity. When we are consistent with what we say we believe and with how we live out that belief, then we have integrity. Consistency between what we say we believe and what we do is so important. I have said many times that if I could boil it all down to one thing my parents did right, it was that they were consistent. What they said they believed on Sunday, they lived out on Monday. The lack of consistency and integrity messes up lives. Perfection is not what the world is looking for; but most people are looking for those with integrity who seek to be pure and holy vessels for God. People are drawn to those whom they can trust and to those who try to live out what they believe. When our lives are clear of the debris, then we are able to make a difference in the world where God has placed us.

DECISION MAKING

"Then we will no longer be little children, tossed by the waves and blown around by every wind of teaching, by human cunning with cleverness in the techniques of deceit" (Eph 4:14). This verse follows Paul's discussion on the body of Christ. He states that we are to "walk worthy of the calling you have received, with all humility and gentleness, with patience, accepting one another in love, diligently keeping the unity of the Spirit with the peace that binds us" (Eph 4:1b-3). He goes on to say that gifts of the Spirit were given to us "for the training of the saints in the work of ministry, to build up the body of Christ" (Eph 4:12). When we are growing believers, we are no longer infants and so are not going to be tossed back and forth by the waves and blown here and there by the wind. I often see

Christian women who are blown by the wind rather than led by the Spirit.

First of all, there are those who change their minds constantly. It has a lot to do with emotions and feelings. It can have a lot to do with having too many irons in the fire. The truth that I can base this on is that God does not change. Numbers 23:19 is just one of many Scripture references that state this is true: "God is not a man who lies, or a son of man who changes His mind. Does He speak and not act, or promise and not fulfill?"

If God does not change His mind, then why do we as women feel it is OK constantly to change our minds depending on our emotions or feelings? We need to sit down and really spend time with the Father, hear His voice, and follow through on what He tells us to do. If we have not met with God on a subject, then we need to do so. Many women wait to see how they feel before they make a decision. That is why men see us as being wishy-washy. How would we feel if every other day God changed His mind on what He had planned for us? It is amazing to me that anyone ever takes women seriously.

Not only do many of us change our minds, but sometimes we avoid the whole thing by not making a decision. The classic example goes something like this: I call a woman to lead a workshop at a conference. She needs time to pray about it and work out the details; that is a given. She can't decide what she's going to speak on. The message I have given is clear that I must know a certain amount of time in advance and that I will need her title, description, and handouts by a designated date. Now I want us to remember that God does or does not want her to speak, and if He does, then He already knows on what she is to speak and what she will need. When she does not have her information ready, she tries to convince me that God has not told her yet. It is not God's fault. It is hers. The problem is that she has not spent time with God on that subject long enough to get with His plan. We should not be tossed by the wind or blown by the waves. We need to sit with God, get His plan, commit to it, and go with it.

Second, many women tend to feel without thinking. Sometimes we even talk without thinking. We are blown by the circumstances around us. We may say, feel, and even do whatever comes to our minds. That puts us on shaky ground and can create a storm of its own. Without time spent with the Lord on a daily basis, we leave our lives subject to the winds that blow by. Some of these winds can be cool and even fun. We have not gotten God's perspective on the situation because we are caught up in the emotion of the whole thing. Unless we have anchored ourselves to the Rock of Christ, we will be blown and tossed in every direction. If the only way the enemy can get to us is to blow us around a little bit, we can bet that He will.

The lack of self-esteem is another reason women are wishy-washy. Women can feel a strong sense of inadequacy and therefore change their tune with every passing wind. Look at the fashion trends out there. The fashion industry tells you that reds are back in style, and what does everyone do? They run out and buy something red. What does God think about that? Well, He hasn't changed on the subject. The bottom line is, you won't know until you sit down and ask Him. You won't know until you are more concerned with what God thinks than what man thinks. Look at Galatians 1:10: "For am I now trying to win the favor of people, or God? Or am I striving to please people? If I were still trying to please people, I would not be a slave of Christ." We must ask God to help us not to be tossed by the winds of fashion or the winds of the world but be led by the Spirit of God to please Him alone. When we tap into His purpose for our lives, we learn that we can be secure in Him.

BALANCE

The Proverbs 31 woman represents the ideal woman. She is balanced in every area of her life. She makes time for herself, her husband, and her children. She makes sure that they are fed and have clothes to keep them warm. She gets up early, works all day, and stays up late into the night. She does all kinds of things, and yet she cannot possibly have done them all at once. She has to have balance in her life.

One of the problem areas for women today is balance. Women tend to wear lots of hats: daughter, sister, friend, mother, grandmother, aunt, worker, carpool driver, and the list goes on. We must keep our hat boxes with us at all times because we never know when we will need a different hat than the one we have on. It takes balance to keep everything going. I always try to remember that balance is tension between the sides. We must make sure our priorities are in order and keep God's perspective at the forefront to make sure that we make the right decisions. Our families must come first. We must always make time for them and for their needs. If other things seem to be taking this time away, then we must reevaluate everything.

For those of us who work outside the home, this becomes a most challenging task. I am thankful that I was able to stay home with my daughter until she started kindergarten. Even then the church was most understanding and encouraging about my needing to keep my home priorities in order. By the time I began traveling for the North American Mission Board (NAMB), I was able to work from the house and was home much more than I was away. God has been gracious to provide working situations where I could do this, and my husband has been the ultimate encourager and supporter. I realize that there will be days when balance seems to be an unachievable goal, but God will make a way and will always be there to help us stay balanced. Every day we must seek God and His wisdom to stay balanced and focused. Those who do not stay balanced will come apart at the seams. To be in ministry means that we must stay balanced in our lives.

RELATIONAL NETWORKING

An important aspect in women's leadership is the relationships and networking that happen. Women are relational people. They are people who genuinely care about others and want to know them. They realize that God brings people into their lives for a reason and that there are no chance meetings. They understand the value of knowing where someone is coming from and understanding what their motivation is. For a woman to be a successful leader, to really make a difference, she has to value relationships and networking.

Some time ago I read a story in the newspaper concerning a new CEO of a Fortune 500 company who happened to be a woman. She spent the first six months of her tenure visiting all the offices around the world and getting to know the employees. She knew the value of relationships and relational networking. For the employees to trust her, they needed to know her.

I learned about relational networking by doing all those odd jobs (most of them for free) around the church. I did not set out to be so relational, but God certainly sent me in that direction. By the time I went on full-time staff and finally got to go to the big staff meeting, just about everyone in the room felt that they had contributed to my getting there. I will always remember my first staff meeting in the Harbor at First Houston and them going around the room, each taking credit for their part in my upbringing. Do you know the best part about it? They were all right. They had helped me grow and develop and had endured the moments of an overexcited housewife who wanted to see others come to Christ. That day forever sealed it in my mind that relationships are everything and that I had better remember that.

We must mention another important truth in relationships. Good relationships mean that I give credit where credit is due. It means that I want the best for those with whom I am working. It means that we are in it together and that I am to encourage, build up, and be the example for those with whom I work. If someone does not get along with me, then I must take the responsibility to take the high road and strive to get along with him or her. If I offend someone, I must go to him or her for forgiveness. If someone is offended by me, then I still must go to this person. It means that there is no room for jealousy, envy, or one-upmanship. It calls for me to be above board and always to look at the best in people. It means being a team member and a team leader. It demands that I do not go around people but I go through them. It is the realization that I can be replaced. It is staying on my face before God and knowing that He cares about relationships and working together. And most of all, for me, it is praising Him on a daily basis that He is the very reason I am going to make a difference at all. Basically, it is not about us. Far too many women decide that they are due the leadership position and that they are out to take it—regardless of the relationships that are at stake.

MENTORING

One of the keys that we see in the Christian world as well as the secular world is the need for women to be mentored. We see this as a biblical concept in Titus 2 but we also see it throughout the Word of God. "Therefore encourage one another and build each other up as you are already doing" (1 Thess 5:11).

As we think about this last challenge that women have in the workplace, mentoring is at the top of the list. It is difficult to find women to be mentors and help those who are coming behind them. In the secular world there are many books written on this. Women who finally make it to a position of influence tend to want to stay there and are threatened that someone else will take their place of leadership. This makes it difficult for young leaders to find mentors, even in the Christian community. Therefore, we must strive to find people to teach us, and we must strive to be mentors and encouragers to others who are coming behind us.

As I reflect over my years in ministry, there were several godly women who mentored me in so many ways. I remember my Sunday school teacher as a young married woman who stuck with me and taught me what it meant to be still before the Lord. I remember the one who encouraged me by always taking my needs to the Father in prayer, and I remember those who, just as a need was expressed, showered their wisdom on me in little bits and pieces. I did not have just one mentor; I had many. If you are in need of a mentor, look for women who could help you in one area. One of my bosses in interior design taught me always to call the smartest person you know when you have a question. I have made that a policy, and it has proven to be so beneficial. Every woman will not know something about every subject. I have also found that the men in my life have been excellent mentors, especially in the area of ministry. I wish there had been women doing women's ministry to whom I could refer over the years, but they were few and far between. Godly men, their wives, and other women have filled in the gap, and as always, God provided the wisdom that I needed at the time I needed it.

One of the things that I have sought to do is to mentor those whom the Lord brings across my pathway. As I am involved in a ministry from coast to coast, one can imagine that I am not always with the same women on a weekly basis, so I look for women into whom I may pour my life. These are usually young women who feel that God is calling them into the ministry. Often I meet them on the campuses of our seminaries or at a conference where I am speaking. I pray that God will send me those who have a passion for Him and want others to know Him. I try to be a listening agent, allow them to share with me their purpose and their dreams, and pray for them. As they share their needs, I can often share some of the wisdom that I have learned from God along the way. I have found that often the questions that I am asked are those about things like balancing my home and work life and other questions about being a godly woman. I always get the questions asking how I got started and how I landed the jobs that I have. (The answer is, staying on my face in prayer and being faithful with small things.) Whatever the question, I have learned that I always have more to learn as well as plenty to share. We need not be intimidated by learning or leading.

IN CONCLUSION

Leading like a godly woman is something we have to strive daily to do. We have to keep in mind that God's principles apply and that we, as women, will have a few things that we need to make sure we are careful about. Being faithful with small things, having passionate aim, taking courageous risks, having integrity, not being wishy-washy, maintaining balance, relational networking, and mentoring are essential ingredients in leadership on which to work. May God make us all into godly women leaders who can make a difference in the world in which He has placed us.

QUESTIONS FOR DISCUSSION

1. From your study on Jesus and how He led with confidence, what are some of the ways we can be confident but remain humble?
2. What are the different roles of leadership held by godly women in Scripture?
3. Look at each of the leadership characteristics of godly women. What are other Scriptures that support each one?
4. Discuss the application of these leadership characteristics in our work in the church. What are the challenges of each one?

Chapter 6

Serving with Men

Jaye Martin

*Whatever you do, do it enthusiastically, as something
done for the Lord and not for men, knowing that you
will receive the reward of an inheritance from the
Lord—you serve the Lord Christ (Col 3:23–24).*

I could not wait to get to staff meeting. I had long
awaited the day that I would be invited. There I sat,
early of course, wide-eyed with my pencil and pad in
hand, just waiting for all the excitement to begin. The staff
arrived and greeted one another, welcomed me to the table, and
there it started. It was much like what anyone would expect in
a meeting—things like opening with prayer requests, sharing
exciting things that God was doing, discussing Sunday's services, reviewing the calendar requests, and various reports from
different ministry areas. At the conclusion of the meeting, the
guys teamed up and went to lunch while the three women in the
room went to a lunch place of our own. I loved every minute of
it. Maybe it was in the weeks to come that the real revelation
began. I was there in every sense of the word, but somehow I felt

invisible. What I said did not seem to be heard. These were incredible men whom to this day I love and respect. They were more than gracious, considerate, and gave every impression of listening to me, but much of what I said did not seem to be understood. Somehow there was this communication gap. One of the most revealing things of all to me was the decisions that were made seemed to be made before the meeting. These guys had connections with one another. Decisions were made at lunch, on the golf course, watching the ball game, and who knows where else. By the time they got to staff meeting, they all seemed to agree. Some weeks a decision would be communicated in the meeting, and by the next week it would have changed. Then one day it hit me. It wasn't that they were leaving me out or trying to keep things from me; there was just a gender difference that I had to figure out.

Men and women working together can be quite a challenge. Even in the best of situations, there are some things that I learned the hard way that I'd like to share. For those of us who find ourselves of the female gender, it is no secret that learning to adapt to a man's world is just an average fact of life. From the moment we are born into this world, the adapting begins. It is not something most of us even think much about; it is simply the way it is. Serving with men in ministry can be an awesome experience. In this chapter we will look at some basics about how men and women are different as well as look at tips for working with the men with whom we serve.

SECULAR STUDIES ON WOMEN AND GENDER

If you have never Googled women's studies before, allow me to be the one to warn you. At the time of this writing, about 152,000,000 sites come up. Add the word *Christian,* and it drops to only 7,590,000. Needless to say, there is quite a bit available if you are interested in researching what the women's secular research has to say, especially on gender differences. Secular women's studies, for the most part, are based on a faulty foundation. They are not built on truth. They are built on studies that claim that males and females are born just alike and that the only difference is the socialization of the genders. What this means is that if you had a baby boy and a baby girl and were able to raise them exactly the same, in the same environment, there would be no differences because of their gender. I cannot help but laugh out loud.

MEN AND WOMEN ARE DIFFERENT

I find it hard to believe that anyone who has seen toddlers playing has not noticed some distinct differences. Usually women who have had both girls and boys are emphatic about the differences between the sexes. I am told that little boys make noises and love to crash things. I know from having a daughter that I did not have to teach her to nurture her stuffed animals or to name each one, dress them up in bows and clothes, and sit them around a little table for a tea party. As we see children growing up, we also see some basic differences between teenage girls and boys. Boys generally like to engage in sports to get to know one another, while girls are usually found sitting and talking. I vividly remember going to an Eagle Scout ceremony of a young man whom my daughter was dating when she was in high school. When he got up to give his speech, one of the things he told was that his best memories of scouting were going to camps where he got to start fires and blow things up. Wow, somehow it never occurred to me that there were camps where young leaders were encouraged to do this. I have to tell you that the scouting trips that I went on were full of making crafts topped off with campfire cooking, singing, and lots of bedtime chats.

It was not too long ago that I heard a young minister preach the evening sermon. He did a wonderful job and told the story of a time when he was growing up. His neighborhood had a tree house, and apparently the neighborhood nearby had just built a new one. Just after he said this, he said, "You know what we had to do?" and then he paused. In my mind I thought, *I guess they went to visit the new tree house to see it.* What he said shocked me (although it should not have). He said, "We had to go and destroy it!" This is just another illustration of how vastly different girls and boys are.

A book I enjoyed reading was John Eldredge's *Wild at Heart*. While not everyone may agree with the whole book, I love his statement inside the front cover: "Deep in his heart, every man longs for a battle to fight, an adventure to live, and a beauty to rescue."[1] He writes of the concept of men being warriors. I do think he is on to something.

As a married adult, I continued to learn about the innate differences. We won't go into all of them, but we lovingly label movies as guy movies or chick flicks. I have almost learned not to talk during the five minutes of the sports news, to do my phone talking and chatting before my husband comes home, and that flowers do not need to be on every piece of upholstery in the house. While my husband is certainly outgoing and a conversationalist, I still talk much more than he does. When he has heard enough, somehow his ears seem to shut down, and he has an ability to see my mouth move and not hear one word that I am saying. I have learned that if I want him to hear me, I had better say it in bite-sized pieces and give the summary version rather than the dissertation version first.

These are just some of the things that women have to learn in order to work with men in the workplace. Regardless of whether they are Christian men and women, there are some differences. Men and women are made in the image of God, and they are, in fact, different. We have already looked at the biblical basis in former chapters so by now we should know that God has a plan, and, as women, we are created uniquely, yet we are equal and important before God. We do need to learn how to work with men so that we can communicate the message that God has given us.

CHRISTIAN WOMEN IN LEADERSHIP

I was blessed to grow up in a Christian home and as a result made a commitment to Christ at a young age. I have been around church since I was in the womb and have lived to see and know many Christian leaders, both male and female. I do remember some early

---

[1] J. Eldredge, *Wild at Heart: Discovering the Secret of a Man's Soul* (Nashville: Thomas Nelson Publishers, 2001), cover.

conversations with my dad, during the dating years, when he would try to explain to me that men thought differently from women. I just had to take him at his word because it was years before I realized the fullness of that concept.

As a young adult in Houston, I knew that God was calling me into the ministry, and during this time I really began to apply what I had learned growing up and at home with my husband to other men with whom I was now working. I can assure you that had my husband not been my coach on how to work with men I would not be where I am today.

What I began to realize was that I could never seem to get my point across to the men with whom I came in contact. I would go to a retreat where lots of people had accepted Christ and would come back and talk about it, telling all the stories, and often they would look at me like they could not understand a word that I was saying. Their responses would be things like, "Well that's nice. How many did you have?" or "How many decisions were there?" I was so excited and emotional and just overflowing, and they were not getting it. The more I talked, the worse it got. I could always tell they were anxious to get away from me. I finally learned that emotional women are scary creatures to men. I also learned that they wanted the bottom line first and that if they wanted more information, they would ask. They also wanted the facts with little emotion. Men seem to be able to put their emotions in a different compartment. I have spent years trying to master that, and I can assure you that every single boss that I have had can attest to the fact that sometimes the tears do follow me to the office. Separating my emotions, both positive and negative, has always been a challenge.

I realize that a few reading this might not appreciate my putting men and women in categories. I do not intend to do so. This chapter is more about the tendencies of men and women and the acknowledgement that God created us differently. There have been some times in the office when I took on the role of calming down the men and also times when one or more of them has had to pull me down from wanting to climb the highest mountain before I was prepared to do so. At times, we will all defy these differences, but generally the things in this chapter seem to be the things that can be stumbling points in working with the opposite sex.

I like to explain it this way: Men are different from women. Men tend to think and talk, while women tend to share and feel. It is not that men never feel or that women do not think; it is that men usually have a thought and say it, while women feel something and then share their feelings. It does make for interesting conversation and certainly is fertile ground for being misunderstood. In order to handle the differences in not only men and women but people that we work with in ministry, it is important that we begin by remembering some basic principles we find in Scripture.

BIBLICAL REMINDERS

Therefore, God's chosen ones, holy and loved, put on heartfelt compassion, kindness, humility, gentleness, and patience, accepting one another and forgiving one another if anyone has a complaint against another. Just as the Lord has forgiven you, so also you must forgive. Above all, put on love—the perfect bond of unity. And let the peace of the Messiah, to which you were also called in one body, control your hearts. Be thankful. Let the message about the Messiah dwell richly among you, teaching and admonishing one another in all wisdom, and singing psalms, hymns, and spiritual songs, with gratitude in your hearts to God. And whatever you do, in word or in deed, do everything in the name of the Lord Jesus, giving thanks to God the Father through Him (Col 3:12–17).

In every situation we are to put on "heartfelt compassion, kindness, humility, gentleness, and patience," as it says in Colossians 3:12. Sometimes we forget this when working with the opposite sex. We may feel that we are being left out intentionally in things that are going on and decisions that are being made. Maybe there is a decision and nobody asked us. Possibly our viewpoint is not included, and we feel we are justified in how we respond. Whatever the scenario, we are to be loving, caring, patient, kind, and the like. We learn to respond and not to react to things that happen, especially in the office. These things seem to be basic, yet the lack of these basic things can harm our ministry and our effectiveness. I have learned that everyone is not out to get me; in fact, if I feel that someone is, there is usually another whole side to the story. I have learned that it is not that the staff is not supportive of me or the ministry to women as much as sometimes they just don't understand it or what the needs are. These become times when I need to educate them on the issues or the needs at hand. I don't need to get upset or haughty or emotional; I just need to communicate to them in a way that they will understand. Whatever I do, I need to do it in such a way as to glorify God. That can only be done when I begin by making sure that I am Spirit filled on a daily basis. Not only the need but the demand for a daily quiet time is essential in ministry. Without it we focus on everything we think we deserve instead of being humble and realizing that we deserve nothing. We must be servants of all just as Christ served us. Everyone has good and bad days, and it is easier to keep this in perspective when we have taken time to begin the day with God's perspective and His plan for the day and for the ministry.

TIPS FOR WORKING WITH MEN

I do have some tips for working with men that I'd love to share with you. I am not going to say that this is an exhaustive list, but I will tell you that they are the things that I have had to learn the hard way. While doing research in this area, I have found that many women make some of these same mistakes. These are things that will be good for all of us to remember.

LET HIM BE YOUR WARRIOR OR YOUR ADVOCATE

What do men love to do? They love to rescue women—the damsel in distress, if you will. I'm still not too sure about why, but there is apparently something in most men that they want to fix things and make everything right again. If there is a woman who is in need, then there is something in his manhood that loves to help and rescue the poor thing. I have often laughed at the men on the airplane who will jump to help the cute young thing who needs help with her luggage. I have also noticed that they will also jump to help any woman who will allow herself to be helped. Now considering I am usually lugging way too much around and often need help, I decided a long time ago that if a man (or anyone) would like to help me, I would just allow it. I may be known for being self-sufficient, but let's face it, why turn down good help? I don't have to be a "do it by myself" girl.

This same principle holds true in the office. When we have a problem or legitimate need, we should go to our boss and tell him the need. I don't think we should run to him with everything, but there are times when he can help. No matter who my boss was, I found that he was always ready to help me and, in fact, to be my warrior. There are times when men can fight the battles for us that we can't. I believe that in general men listen more to other men, and there are times when he can make things happen when we cannot. Let your boss be your warrior or your advocate.

Relationships Are Essential

Developing relationships in the workplace is very important. I believe that women are mysterious to men. They don't quite understand us or know how to act or what to do with us. I sat by a man on the airplane the other day, and for no reason he began to tell me about his boss (who is a woman) and ask me questions about how to work with her. I chose to listen because he really did need to talk about his situation. He said that his greatest frustration was that sometimes she acted like a man and sometimes she acted like a woman. He said that one minute she was all hard and tough and did not want to talk to him, and the next minute she was all weepy and talking in circles. He wondered what he was supposed to do with that. I feel quite sure that many men have wondered the same thing. He just wanted her to be "normal." The conversation was a vivid reminder that as women we need to develop normal relationships with the guys in the office. We need to learn to get to know them and work with them. We must be human and relational and be godly women in all our dealings. I have found that briefly asking about their families lets them know that I respect their home life. Asking questions and allowing them to mentor me in some areas shows that I am teachable. We must not just talk to them when we need something but be genuinely interested in the things in which they are interested. Developing relationships with the men we work with is most helpful in ministry.

PROTECT YOUR WARRIOR AND THE BABIES

Our warriors or advocates will protect us, but we need to return the favor. When someone makes a negative comment about our boss, we need to defend him. It may be that the pastor has made a decision with which someone is unhappy. Even if we agree with the criticism, we must learn to respect the decision and show respect for the one who made it. We must be supportive of our bosses. It is best to respond to the person by reminding her that we do not have all the information and that she needs to address personally the one who made the decision. I have found that people generally just like to complain to someone. Seldom do they go to the person anyway. We should make sure that we are protecting those with whom we serve.

Another issue here is to protect those who serve under us in areas of leadership. I know that when working with women there are times when one will complain about another. We must not join the complaint bandwagon. Encourage the one complaining to go to the woman personally just as it says in Matthew 18. Sometimes there will be a legitimate complaint, and it might be that you need to get the other side on the issue. As we are all aware, there are many versions to any situation, and we are only hearing one. Regardless of what might need to be addressed, encourage biblical interaction and protect those who serve under you.

Listen More Than You Talk

As women who love to talk, it is important that we are quieter around the men. I am not saying not to be yourself or never to engage in conversation; I am saying that for many women in ministry, we need to learn when to listen and when to speak. We should learn to listen and hear the whole story from our bosses. We must learn not to interrupt. We must also learn that those who listen can come across as being very wise. There is a time to speak and a time to listen. We must be sure that we are listening to what others are saying rather than making our list of what we want to say at the next available moment.

Talk in Bullets

I have found that I can usually tell whether an e-mail is from a man or a woman by the length of it. Most of my e-mails from my bosses have been one to three words. It is amazing how much they can say with so few words. E-mails from the women whom I serve with seem to be longer. It is equally amazing how many pages someone needs to say one basic thing. Because of the national ministry that I am blessed to have, I get numerous e-mails from women, and so there are times when I have to read an e-mail several times to determine what the lady is really saying. When we work with men, we need to learn to talk in bullets with as few words as possible to communicate our thoughts. I have found it helpful on e-mails to write out what I want to say, tweak it, and then summarize it with a word or two and send it as a heading. I write the bottom line or bullet first, and then put phrases or bullets of explanation for them so that if they need more information, they can read it. Somehow this satisfies my need to communicate more than the base facts and their need to have the bottom line or bullet first. If I am going to talk to my boss about an idea that I have for ministry, I try to talk through that idea with other women first. This helps me think through the idea, and then I try to come up with a short phrase to communicate the idea. With many men it is even helpful to write the idea on paper using headings and bullets. This way, even when we do talk in circles, they understand better what we are telling them or asking about.

Show Him Respect

Respect is something that every man needs. It is easy to show respect for men by listening, not rolling our eyes, watching our tone of voice, and general things that we know but may not do. We also show respect by not nagging or treating him like an idiot. Some may be wondering why I would need to bring these things up, but apparently women must tend not to be respectful because men keep noting these things as problems. We should respect our fathers, husbands, and all the men with whom we work. We must treat them like we would treat Christ, regardless of how we feel or how they treat us. Most men respond well to those who show them respect.

Birth Things and Grow Them Up

In the church many things need to be done, and often the ministry to women can help by starting new ministries, growing them up, and sending them out for the whole church. Where I served, there was a lady who had a passion for prayer. She went to some prayer conferences, learned how to teach others, and began a prayer ministry. It wasn't long before that ministry became churchwide and came under a different staff person. We also had a lady who wanted to offer support groups for women. There were groups for codependency, balance, and abused women, among others. These groups were reaching so many, and the men wanted to be a part of them. We had grown the ministry to the point where it needed to come under the direction of the counseling pastor so that the whole church body could benefit.

I meet many women's ministry leaders who want to start ministries but want to keep them. They feel that just about everything should come under the women's ministry team. The purpose of the ministry is to support the church and the needs as a whole. If the women's team can see a need and fill it, that is wonderful. When the new ministry is ready to be sent out, then it needs to be released. Those with whom we work appreciate it when we are serving the whole church and giving in ministry for the good of all.

BE AN INFLUENCER—YOU DON'T HAVE TO GET THE CREDIT

One of the joys of being a leader and a woman is that of knowing that we have been an influence. I have found it is more important that something happens than who gets credit for it. I have heard many women say that they have an idea and no one listens to them. Then a few months pass, and the pastor comes up with the same idea, and he gets the credit for it. What difference does it make? Is it not God who gave the idea to begin with? I like the fact that I can influence decisions and don't have to get the credit for things. It is fun just to know that God is using us and our ideas.

This same principle applies to those who serve with us. We need to give them the credit where credit is due. When we lift up others, it comes back in return. We do not need to be concerned about who did or came up with what but give all the glory to God and thank Him for allowing us to be involved in the process.

BE A TEAM PLAYER

I think that I have been able to learn this by watching the men interact. Have you ever noticed that the men seem to respect and respond to whoever the leader is? They seem to have more of a pack mentality. They expect someone to lead, and they act like a team and follow the one in charge. Even if they disagree, the way they get ahead is to work harder and be even more of a team player.

Being a team player means that we play our positions and we play them well. It is all about the team and God, the ultimate coach. Sports have a clear set of rules and positions for the players. Somehow, as women, we are not content just to play our positions well; we want to jump ahead and score and get all the credit. When there are clear rules, we want to be the exception. We want things to revolve around us, whether we intend it or not. Especially in ministry we need to learn to be team players and play for the good of the whole.

DON'T RESCUE EVERYONE ELSE

Men may like to fix things, but women like to fix people. Working with men and with the team means that we must not try to fix those with whom we serve; neither must we try to fix the flaws that might linger in their ministries. In my early years of ministry, I spent way too much time trying to help every ministry area to be perfect. I thought that if we had a perfect church, then more people would come to know the Lord. I learned that I need to fix and deal with the log in my own ministries and let others deal with areas with which I should not be concerned. We come across as the critical spirit when we try to fix every flaw that is out there. When we do this, no one wants to be around us. We need to learn to deal with our own areas and not try to rescue everyone else's.

DON'T GO OVER HIS HEAD—STAY UNDER AUTHORITY

Have you ever watched women? They seem to want to get ahead by jumping outside the system. Instead of becoming the ideal team player and working together, they desire to show how much harder they work, and they often go around their bosses to those over them and pat themselves on the back. It is amazing that we are still living out the same problem Eve had. We must watch and be careful that we are being a part of the team and that we are staying under authority. This can be a challenge in a small group when we are working with the pastor's wife and we know everyone. We must be careful to discuss the appropriate things with the appropriate person at the appropriate time. I know there have been many times when I heard about something that was coming down the pike long before my bosses did, yet I had to sit on it and be careful with the information. Many times I knew that a phone call to the top would correct the situation, but it would also ruin every relationship in between. When we go around our bosses, we show disrespect for the authority under which God has placed us. As women, this is an area on which we all need to continue to work.

Leave Your Emotions at Home

I wish that I had mastered the tears by now. I remember how many times I would get teary eyed in staff meeting when someone would talk about people coming to know the Lord or about someone losing a loved one. I remember praying, and my voice cracking as I prayed over difficult situations. In a roomful of women, we can find forgiveness. In a roomful of men, I am not so sure. One of my bosses told me that he noticed that I was fine until I had to respond about a difficult situation, and he suggested that I just sit and not feel that I had to respond when I felt emotional on a need or an issue. These were wise words and helped me greatly. He felt that I was not taken seriously because of my tears, and he was right. At that time I also learned that cutting the sugar and the caffeine was most helpful to me as well. Whatever works for us, we need to do.

Appropriate Nesting

One of the things my husband taught me was that men don't trust women who don't nest in their offices. As an attorney he has worked with many women attorneys. He says he always knows whether she is a long-timer or a short-timer by whether she nests in the office. Since I have had offices in buildings in other states, I have made it a point to make sure I move my personal items like photos, diplomas, and work-related things into the offices so that there would be no question as to my "being there." I want my office to look like my office even when I am far away.

One of the mistakes that I have seen women make is nesting too much. What I mean by that is making the office look more like their bedroom rather than like an office and living room. Certainly it is appropriate to have nice, female things in the office. However, do leave the lace and the glowing, scented candles at home. We don't want the office to smell like perfume; it is a work environment. I have heard the response that the men get to have deer heads hanging so why would we not be able to have our pink cushions with the cute bows, but that becomes another story. If I were writing a book for men, I might have a comment. From our standpoint, however, they can have their animal heads, but we still don't get to go crazy with the frills. I will admit to having a mantle and candles in my Louisville office, but I can assure you that nothing is burning.

BE A GODLY WOMAN IN YOUR ATTITUDE, DRESS, AND ACTIONS

Act, dress, and live with an attitude that will honor Christ. In this day and age, we have completely forgotten some basic things. I am not talking about styles or trends; I am talking about some things like necklines and pants that are too low, hemlines that are too high, clothes that are too tight, and flirty attitudes that need to be left at home. I am amazed at the Christian women's conferences that I attend where women, even speakers, wear necklines that would distract even women. If there are "cracks" in the front or the back, they need to be covered. That is it. Case closed. It is inappropriate. We need to model the behavior of godly women at church and in the neighborhood—how we dress and how we act. This means that we are careful about things like eating a meal with a male, meeting behind closed doors, riding in the car with the opposite sex, and the like. It only takes one accusation from someone to ruin our ministries. We have to think about how others will see us and what they might think. When I have defied these truths, I have regretted it. Years ago I allowed a young man to go on church visits with me. I was twice his age. When my birthday came, I received flowers and had to call him and make sure he understood the boundaries and apologize for not finding a man with whom he could go. We do this to protect ourselves but also to protect others. Yes, it can be inconvenient. Yes, there are times when someone will send a car to pick me up somewhere, and I need to ride with them. In most cases, however, these are things that can be addressed early on, and most of us in the ministry are very careful to make sure to avoid these situations.

Neither is there any room for even the slightest flirtation in the office. We must be careful not to touch the men with whom we work. We also have to watch what we say because they may take it in a way that is completely different from how we meant it. I am not a "huggy" person, but many people, men and women, are. I am careful to do the sideways hug with men if they approach me, and I try to stick to the handshakes, high fives, or pats on the shoulder. I have found that taking a step backward sends the signal that I am uncomfortable if someone is being inappropriate. I have also found that a stern eyeball-to-eyeball stare can communicate volumes to remarks that never should have been made. We want to be women, but we want to be godly in our interactions in ministry.

IN CONCLUSION

Serving with men is a great experience. Most often they say what they mean and don't have a hidden agenda. Respect them and serve them faithfully, and they will be your advocates at every turn. I thank God for the awesome men with whom I have served and who have tolerated me while I learn to communicate and strive to be that professional, godly woman that we all long to be.

QUESTIONS FOR DISCUSSION

1. Based upon your reading of Colossians 2:12–17, what are the concepts that can be applied regarding working with men?
2. Review the list of tips for working with men. How can women apply each one?
3. What are some of the struggles that women may have had working with men? What is an appropriate way to deal with or minimize those struggles?
4. What are some problems that could potentially happen in ministry settings between men and women? How should each be handled?
5. Search the Scriptures for other passages that can be applied to men and women serving together.

Part Three:
The Tasks of Women's Ministry
What Do We Do?

THE GREAT COMMISSION

*Then Jesus came near and said to them, "All authority
has been given to Me in heaven and on earth. Go,
therefore, and make disciples of all nations, baptizing
them in the name of the Father and of the Son and of
the Holy Spirit, teaching them to observe everything I
have commanded you. And remember, I am with you
always, to the end of the age" (Matt 28:18–20).*

THE GREAT COMMANDMENT

*He said to him, "You shall love the Lord your God
with all your heart, with all your soul, and with all
your mind. This is the greatest and most important
commandment. The second is like it: Love your*

neighbor as yourself. All the Law and the Prophets depend
on these two commandments" (Matt 22:37–40).

TITUS 2

In the same way, older women are to be reverent in behavior,
not slanderers, not addicted to much wine. They are to teach
what is good, so that they may encourage the young women
to love their husbands and children, to be sensible, pure,
good homemakers, and submissive to their husbands, so
that God's message will not be slandered (Titus 2:3–5).

Now that we know why and who, we need to know what we need to do to plug women into the life of Christ in the local church. This section introduces us to the purpose and specifically the tasks of the ministry to women in the local church. The function of the church is taken from the Great Commission and the Great Commandments. This is where we understand the functions of evangelism, discipleship, ministry, worship, and fellowship. We begin with worship. We worship individually, and we worship collectively and corporately as the whole church body comes together. We share Christ by doing evangelism and missions. We disciple new believers, grow them up in the faith, and involve them in ministry through spiritual gifts and the use of their talents. Our fellowship flows out of serving together.

The tasks of women's leadership and ministry are a support to the overall purpose and function of the church. Therefore, the tasks of ministry to women are to reach women for Christ (chap. 7), nurture them in the faith (chap. 8), involve them in ministry (chap. 9), engage the next generation (chap. 10), and support the church family (chap. 11). These tasks flow from the Great Commission (evangelism, discipleship, ministry), the Great Commandment (love God and love others), and Titus 2 (engage the next generation).

94

In this section we will not look at "how to do" these things as much as "what we need to do" from the biblical perspective. There are several practical books on programs that women's ministries can implement, and these are readily available. Here, we chose to look at the functions more from a philosophical standpoint of what needs to be done than from how it needs to happen. We have found that too many ministries are starting programs and studies without understanding what God's intention is for the women of the church. Our attempt is not to stop the programs but rather to encourage pastors and women's leaders to ask the hard questions such as, "Is this program, study, or event fulfilling the God-given tasks of a ministry to women?" For instance, we may love to pull a Bible study and DVD off the shelf of a bookstore for a group of women, but is this study fulfilling the need to reach, disciple, and involve these women in ministry? Maybe there is a retreat the church has always done. The question is, What is the purpose of the retreat, and is the purpose serving to accomplish one or more of the tasks of ministry to women? If the purpose of the retreat is fellowship, then we have missed the point. The purpose includes evangelism, discipleship, ministry, engaging the next generation, and supporting the church. Fellowship is something that flows out of ministering. Fellowship happens when women come together to do evangelism, discipleship, and ministry. Fellowship, as we see in Acts, is the result of serving the church together. We are not advocating that churches need to quit having retreats for women; we are advocating that churches need to get back to the biblical basis of what a ministry to women should look like.

The chapters in this section will help the leaders of the ministry to women know what they are called to do in order to fulfill and support the life of the church.

Chapter 7

REACH
Women for Christ

Jaye Martin

*Then Jesus came near and said to them, "All authority has
been given to Me in heaven and on earth. Go, therefore, and
make disciples of all nations, baptizing them in the name of
the Father and of the Son and of the Holy Spirit, teaching them
to observe everything I have commanded you. And remember,
I am with you always, to the end of the age" (Matt 28:18–20).*

MAKING YOUR WOMEN'S MINISTRY EVANGELISTIC

Since the purpose of the church is comprised of evangelism,
discipleship, ministry, worship, and fellowship, then it stands
to reason that ministry to women in the church includes these
things as well. Aside from corporate worship, the way we live out
our lives is by sharing Christ, discipling others, and doing the ministry of the church. The *koinonia* fellowship of the New Testament
flows out of doing these things to the glory of God. In this chapter

we will focus on reaching women and sharing the good news of Christ with them. How do we make our ministry to women evangelistic? Not only do we reach out to those within our church walls, we also reach out to those in our families, neighborhoods, communities, workplaces, cities, states, and countries for the cause of Christ. The Great Commission is given to each of us, whether we find it easy or not. God gives this command to every believer, but He never intended us to do the huge task alone.

WOMEN WHERE YOU LIVE

Women of all types are just waiting for someone to care about them. They need the love of Christ, and as Christian women in leadership we need to find them and share the good news. Look at just some of the women whom you might find in your hometown.

Laura has a job at the town diner. She got pregnant in high school, was married after the baby came, and already at the age of 19 finds herself a single mom. She works at the diner every day until about 9:00 p.m. while her mom watches her toddler. Sundays are a busy workday so church is not an option for her. She wants to study at the community college but can never find the energy to go over to check out her options. Laura spends every waking minute either working or caring for her child. Laura is desperate for adult relationships and longs for a reason to keep going on.

Then there is Yosheka. Yosheka feels like she was born working. As the daughter of a working mom who could hardly pay the bills, Yosheka had to work odd jobs during high school years to help out at home. She worked her way through the local college while she lived at home and was the first in her family to go to college and finish. She got a job at the insurance company and works full days. At night she has to help with younger brothers and sisters while her mom works the night shift. Yosheka continues to have interest from young men, but none have treated her like a lady and she finds herself in a cycle of bad relationships that she finds hard to break. She'd love some wisdom and direction but has no idea where to go, nor does she have the extra money to spend to get the help she needs. She has a church she claims but never seems to make it to the services so she resorts to the TV pastor who continues to tell her that she is an overcomer.

Meet Sajal. She's one of a large family of religious believers who worship just about everything. In her home are grandparents as well as aunts and uncles who share the house. Sajal is married with two grade-school girls who go to the public school. When the girls aren't at school, she is busy doing her part of the homemaking responsibilities. She loves her family but would love to meet some other moms and learn a little more about the culture in which she now finds herself living.

Becky lives there too. Becky is married and appears to have the perfect home situation, but it is not. Becky's husband makes plenty of money so they live in a huge house and the kids go to private school. Her husband travels most of the time, leaving Becky with lots of free time. She volunteers at charities and is a good person. She spends her days going from the charities to the mall and to her many beauty appointments.

Maria loves to cook so her home is always full of neighborhood kids who come and go. She's a sweet woman who is overcome with so much depression that she appears shy and introverted. Her family keeps growing with kids and grandkids, and she rarely has a minute for herself. She wonders if God is real and would like to know anything about Him. She has a church but she doesn't go much, and when she does, they don't teach anything about the Bible.

Roberta lives alone. Her husband died a few years ago, and it is hard for her to see to drive at night. Her TV is her constant companion because her children are grown and live far away. They are busy so they rarely call. Many of her friends are in retirement homes or have moved to live with their children. She knows the postman, the grocery manager, and the lady across the street. Other than that, she's pretty much on her own.

These are just a few of the women in your community. Each of them desperately needs Jesus.

EVANGELISM AND MISSIONS DEFINED

Let's begin by defining evangelism and missions. Evangelism is sharing the good news of Jesus Christ in the power of the Holy Spirit and leaving the results to God. Missions is where you take the sharing of the good news. Many define missions as crossing cultural boundaries. It is interesting that the Bible does not separate evangelism and missions, but so many church and denomination structures do. This should never be the case. Scripturally, you should not have one without the other. I like to describe evangelism as what you say (the talking) and missions as where you go (the walking). So, for the purpose of this chapter, I am putting the two back where they should be: together. Evangelism is sharing the good news of Christ with the world. The Great Commission is found in all four Gospels and in Acts. It is clear. We are to go (ministry), make disciples (discipleship) of all nations (crossing cultures / missions), and baptize (share Christ and celebrate through believers' baptism) them in the name of God the Father, the Holy Spirit, and Jesus Christ. There is no other name whereby one can be saved. Jesus said, "I am the way, the truth, and the life. No one comes to the Father except through Me" (John 14:6).

The world in which we live is not the world in which our parents lived or the world in which we grew up. Just in the last 10 years, the Internet has brought the world into our homes. Those who know nothing beyond their communities have now seen the world without traveling anywhere. The Internet has brought in the good with the bad. We are a global society, and it is just as natural today to talk to someone in Asia as it is to talk to someone next door—in fact, more likely. We communicate through cell phones, e-mails, texting, and podcasts and are more likely to connect through these instruments than we are face-to-face. All of this has brought people closer together yet has separated them farther apart. Communities are increasingly important, and companies who have mastered community have risen to the top of the market.

The challenges of communicating the message of Christ are in one sense difficult yet in another sense easier than ever. Women are lost and hurting and alone. They are in broken relationships. They are in desperate need of the ultimate relationship that Christ offers, and yet they usually don't even know it. The world has offered them cheap thrills and empty promises, and they have bought into it all. In Paul's writings in 2 Timothy 3, we see a picture of lostness. It could have been written last week:

> *But know this: difficult times will come in the last days. For people will be lovers of self, lovers of money, boastful, proud, blasphemers, disobedient to parents, ungrateful, unholy, unloving, irreconcilable, slanderers, without self-control, brutal, without love for what is good, traitors, reckless, conceited, lovers of pleasure rather than lovers of God, holding to the form of religion but denying its power. Avoid these people! For among them are those who worm their way into households and capture idle women burdened down with sins, led along by a variety of passions, always learning and never able to come to a knowledge of the truth (2 Tim 3:1–7).*

How do we begin to reach women for Christ? It begins with prayer.

PRAYER

> *When they had prayed, the place where they were assembled was shaken, and they were all filled with the Holy Spirit and began to speak God's message with boldness (Acts 4:31).*

We begin to make our ministry to women evangelistic with prayer. God promises that He will be with us. God wants people to be saved more than we do. He wants to use us in His great work. His intention is not that we walk around with great guilt or a burden but for us to rely on Him and let Him show us the way. After all, as crazy as it might seem to us, this is His plan and what an honor for Him to include us in the greatest miracle of life—that of another person being transformed and coming to Christ.

Numerous aspects of prayer are important. You can read books and do studies on prayer, but the key is to pray. This concept is novel, I know, but true. We begin to pray by praying for ourselves. We pray that we might be open to God and to His plan. We pray that our hearts might be pure and that we would see the opportunities He brings before us. We pray for our church and our ministries that we might become the holy, pure, unblemished, and productive bride of Christ. We pray that our ministries might live out the purpose of the church and that they might not be self-serving but be self-sacrificing. We pray specifically for unbelievers. Not just, "God, save Laura," but "God, open Laura's heart to You, remove the barriers that are causing her not to see You, and draw her to Yourself." We pray the Scriptures for our friends and family members who do not know Christ personally. We pray that they might seek God and seek the truth that will set them free. We pray for them by name. Prayer opens our hearts to the heart of God. Prayer puts everything back in God's control and brings God's perspective. Prayer opens the door for us to right our own relationship with Him so that He can more effectively flow through us with the power of the Holy Spirit.

Sin separates us from God. When we have unconfessed sin, we cannot see or hear God as clearly because our wrongdoing blocks the flow of God's voice. It is not that God cannot still speak to us but that He has a harder time getting through to us. When we have confessed our sins, we are pure and clear, and we are able to hear Him. God wants people to be saved more than we do. He desires to use us and can do so most effectively when we are clean before Him.

We make time for personal prayer every day and specifically in praying for the lost. Then we lead our leaders to pray and to pray together for people by name to come to faith. God honors corporate prayer. He honors leaders coming together to pray. Not only does He honor personal prayer and the prayers of leaders; He also honors the prayers of women coming together and praying in larger groups. It is vital to make prayer the foundation for ministry.

Over the years of ministry, I have learned time and time again that there is always time for prayer. On those occasions when I thought that we did not have time to pray, I lived to regret it. I found that when I began a meeting with heartfelt prayer God honored the time and multiplied it. He always blessed and helped us focus on what was most important. When I rushed into a meeting with a quick prayer to begin, the meeting seemed never to end. It always took longer, and many things were left unresolved. But when I began with prayer and allowed God to move, the agenda just seemed to flow. God honors private and corporate prayer for the lost.

MODEL

A disciple is not above his teacher, but everyone who
is fully trained will be like his teacher (Luke 6:40).

We see in Scripture that Jesus *was* the message. He modeled what He taught. He lived out what He said to do. While this is true in every area of life, it is essential in sharing Christ. As leaders, we model how to share Christ. It is great to enlist someone who will lead in the area of evangelism and reaching women, but it does not excuse us from doing it ourselves. The women in our ministry will look just like we do. They will emphasize what we emphasize and devalue what we devalue. Just take a look in the mirror. How many times did you tell yourself that you were not going to act like your mother and then you acted like her anyway? If you have children, then you know that they may pick up your good traits, but typically they pick up and seem to magnify your bad ones. In many ways we act just like our parents, and our children act just like us. If we want our church and our ministries to reach people for Christ, we live out reaching people before them. We show them the way. None of us have arrived, so if we need to come before our women and admit that evangelism is our weakness, then by all means we confess this to God and to them, get it over with, and we learn together how to reach women for the cause of Christ. The Holy Spirit will give us the words to say when we need them (Luke 12:11–12).

ENLIST

> *But as for you, continue in what you have learned*
> *and firmly believed, knowing those from whom you*
> *learned, and that from childhood you have known*
> *the sacred Scriptures, which are able to instruct*
> *you for salvation through faith in Christ Jesus. All*
> *Scripture is inspired by God and is profitable for*
> *teaching, for rebuking, for correcting, for training in*
> *righteousness, so that the man of God may be complete,*
> *equipped for every good work (2 Tim 3:14–17).*

In every aspect of ministry, enlisting leaders is important business. In evangelism we enlist leaders who will instruct women in sharing Christ, but we also enlist the women to come and be trained in how to reach people for Christ.

In order to enlist the right leaders, we need to go back and look at chapter 5 again. We want to look for women who are honest and humble, women who have a passion for God and are authentic believers. It is better to have a leader who is willing to admit that she is new at doing evangelism than to have one who acts like she shares her faith but never does. We look for women who are willing to be hands-on leaders who will not only show the women how to share their faith, but women who are willing to tell their stories of their success and their failures in sharing Christ. We look for women who take prayer seriously and who believe that God is still in the saving business. I would rather have a woman who has a passion for the Lord than one who is just showing up to teach another class. It is also important to have teachers who are sensitive to the needs of the class members. I have found that even in churches so many of the women who show up for evangelism training classes are either seekers and do not have a relationship to Christ yet or are women who have family members or close friends who are not believers. When a woman comes to learn evangelism, the instructor makes sure she presents the plan of salvation in such a way that women who are lost will understand the message and choose Christ. It seems that more times than not, someone in a class will come to know the Lord for the first time. This is an exciting time for the class. It is also important for the leader to be sensitive to those in the group who might be married to unbelievers or who have parents or children who are not saved. They often need some coaching on how to live and help with some of the finer points of what it means to be a Christ follower in their home. Many women who come may be new believers themselves and will need someone who will spend a few minutes listening to them and helping them to apply the Scriptures.

Enlistment of the teachers is important, but this is only the beginning of enlistment. Encouraging women to take the class is extremely important as well. Generally announcements can be made and letters and e-mails sent, but a one-on-one invitation will be what brings women into the class. The class is essential but fun. To see someone come to faith in Christ is the most exciting thing in this world, and this needs to be communicated. Testimonies and stories that can be told in other women's classes and at the events will also help in enlisting. Creative titles and a fun atmosphere for learning with lots of interaction will make for an inviting environment. I like to use things like logo pins, scarves, beads, jewelry, and other items for women to wear during the length of the class sessions. This gives interest to other women who see them outside the classroom but makes for a great memory for those in it. It builds team spirit and creates the excitement that something is happening.

TRAIN

And what you have heard from me in the presence
of many witnesses, commit to faithful men who
will be able to teach others also (2 Tim 2:2).

When your leaders have been enlisted, you will want to provide training for them. One of the most common problems in evangelism

104

leadership is that the leaders are just thrown in and expected to know how to train and how to teach. This is seldom the case. Leaders should be trained in a way that gets them involved in the process. Some of the better known evangelism training tools out there require the leader to go through some sort of a certification process. While this may not be necessary, women especially like to go through a training class or workshop before they lead and teach something, especially evangelism. If you are able to train women personally, this is great. If not, set up training or send your teachers to a workshop to be trained where they can have some hands-on involvement and talk through questions that come up. Many denominations offer training on a national, statewide, and local basis so look for opportunities that your church and denominational leaders may know about. If you are using a particular training course, just locate the source and find out what the options for training are in your area.

One of the most effective means of training is when potential leaders are asked to be a part of the class and are trained by being a member. Sometimes during the class sessions a leader will emerge, and this woman can be recruited to serve as an assistant teacher or a co-teacher while she learns the process. If you are offering a new evangelism course at your church, it might be that you can send a leader to another church to be a part of their class. This has also been very beneficial in helping to get leaders trained. Many of the larger churches will be able to assist in helping smaller churches get evangelism training and ministries started.

INVOLVE

Based on the gift they have received, everyone
should use it to serve others, as good managers
of the varied grace of God (1 Pet 4:10).

Involvement is a key factor in every aspect of ministry to women, especially in evangelism. One of the keys to reaching women is to involve women to reach women. The more women that are mobilized, the more that are reached. I have heard the statistic for years that for every one person involved in an effort, they bring three more with them. That means that if you are having an event and you want 100 women to attend, then you will need to involve at least 25 women in the process at some level before the event. That is also true in reaching women. To effectively reach women, you will need to look for ways to involve them. If you are going to host an evangelism training class, then it would be helpful to enlist lots of women to help you to do it. You may only need one teacher and one assistant teacher, but think how many others could be involved if you put in a little effort. You could enlist several women to serve to help at a sign-in table, several to hand out creative flyers or something else that would attract attention, ask some to set up the chairs in the room, make name tags, make coffee, make a fruit tray, bring paper and pencils for everyone, pick up the course books, and the list goes on. One time I had a training event called "Sharing Your Apple." It started on a Wednesday night just after our churchwide supper. During the supper I placed an apple on each table with an invitation to come and bring the apple to the class. We had a huge turnout because it created interest. The apples became an illustration for wanting to be bright, shiny, pure apples for Christ. Involving people and making things fun just takes a little effort but is certainly worth it. Get a group of young creative minds together to help you. The more involved, the more you will have who are ready to share their faith.

REACH

> *So that they might seek God, and perhaps they*
> *might reach out and find Him, though He is*
> *not far from each one of us (Acts 17:27).*

It seems obvious to say that in order to reach women for Christ, we actually have to reach out to those unbelievers whom we know and come across. I meet so many people who say that one of their problems in evangelism is that they just do not know many lost people. No matter who we are or how churched we are, there are many unbelievers all around us. We just have to open our eyes to see them.

One of the easiest places to look for the lost is right within the walls of the church. Look at the church rolls. We are usually surprised that there are people who attend every week who have never made the commitment to follow Christ. They may be married to believers or part of a family who attends so they attend with the family. Over the years I have called many of these people, and often, when they realize that they need to decide personally to follow Christ, they want to do so. Often no one has asked them, and they have just gotten caught up in the system without ever really making a commitment. Many others do believe but have never joined the church family. It is always fun to invite them to a special church baptismal service and turn baptism into a celebration. There will be still others who have visited the church but never followed through. Sometimes they need someone to help them talk through some issues. Women should not feel that they have to have the answers before they start contacting women because a pastor or someone there usually can help with the answers. Loving care is something that we all can do, and we want to let others know that we care about them having an abundant life and about where they will spend eternity. Others right before our eyes are college students, youth, and children. With the massive numbers of broken families today, many children are only able to come once or twice a month. These people are great to follow up on, and the ministry to women can help in the process.

Another group of people to reach out to are work associates. When women work outside the home, there are usually many with whom we work who do not know the Lord. These women are ideal candidates with whom to build relationships. These women can be invited to numerous events and activities that the church and ministry is hosting. Sharing what God is doing in our lives is the best way to start.

Women who are not working for a salary are often involved in numerous community efforts where they meet women who need to know Jesus. Depending on what season of life we are in, there will be lots of ways to meet these women. Community and neighborhood events, school related events, health and fitness centers, even hospitals and health-care facilities are great places to reach out to people.

Many of our own neighbors, friends, and families need to know the Lord. People we meet at grocery stores, dry cleaners, and other places also need to know the Lord. We should always look for ways to build bridges to these people to get to know them.

It is helpful to encourage women to start a list of those whom they know and to begin to pray for each by name. I like to pray that God will give me the opportunity to share with each one and the words to say. I also pray that I will be able to see the opportunity so that I am ready to share when He prompts me to do so.

CELEBRATE

But we had to celebrate and rejoice, because this
brother of yours was dead and is alive again;
he was lost and is found (Luke 15:32).

The celebration of people coming to the Lord is a biblical principle. We need to celebrate the process, celebrate the results, and celebrate with baptism. Every step of people walking toward Christ is important. We should affirm those who ask questions about the Christian life, encourage those who attend our ministry classes and want to be a part of what is happening, and celebrate the whole process of coming to know God personally. When people make a decision, we need to help them grow in the Lord and to be a part of things that will help them in their walk. We also need to work with them and their families to celebrate baptism. I have found that this is a great way for them to communicate their newfound faith in Christ to their family. Baptism is the picture of several things. Picture the baptismal pool as a grave. Baptism is a symbol of Jesus' dying, being buried, and being raised from the dead. It is a testimony of our dying to self, being buried with Christ, and being raised to walk in a new life. It shows that the old life is gone and the new life has begun. When we celebrate baptism and explain it, people want others to come and be a part of it. I have also found that special churchwide baptisms on Easter, Mother's Day, and even other special days are great ways to help people who are waiting baptism to go ahead and join in on the celebration.

SUPPORT

> *So that they would support the people and*
> *the house of God (Ezra 8:36b).*

We will spend a whole chapter on the concept of support, but it is still important to mention here. Support is essential in reaching women for Christ. We support the church body as a whole in evangelism efforts. Encourage women to be involved in the training that the church offers. We can offer training specific to women, but the overall training is important as well. Most of the offerings we do for women will only complement and add to what is offered for the whole church. It is also important to support the pastor and his plan for reaching people for Christ. We make sure we are in line with his vision and are supporting him in every way. For churches with multiple staffs, there may be staff members who have the responsibility to lead evangelism in our churches. It will be important to network with these staff and to make sure we are following their lead. Our training and outreach efforts should complement what they are doing.

Another important area of support is that of church programming. When the church has an Easter presentation of the gospel story, it will be important to offer to help with follow-up of those who come. Other organizations that do outreach are also important to network with. When following up with prospects, it is important that information be shared.

In Summary

Making your women's ministry one that reaches women for Christ is of the utmost importance. Prayer for evangelism, modeling how to reach out, enlisting leaders as well as those to be trained, training, involving women in the process of evangelism, reaching out to women who do not know Christ, celebrating the results, and supporting the church are all just a part of reaching women for Christ.

WOMEN'S EVANGELISM STRATEGIES

To be able to reach women, we develop evangelism strategies. This is one of the greatest disappointments that I see in the Christian community. Often we train women to share the gospel, but we think that is where it ends. Actually, the training is just the beginning. We develop a plan or strategy to reach women for Christ. In Acts 1:8, we clearly see that we are to reach Jerusalem, Judea, Samaria, and the ends of the earth. In our language and setting, that means that we reach our communities, states, country, and all nations. This is something we do all at once. We do this by developing strategic plans and setting up a system. I love the illustration that I heard about harvesting a field. We would never think of harvesting a field by riding the harvester in circles. Harvesting is done with precise plans to harvest every grain. Even when I was in East Asia, those harvesting were doing so by hands and in rows. What a picture of how we need to see evangelism. We reach people one by one, but we also have a plan that will at least give everyone the opportunity to hear the gospel and accept Christ.

Several modes of doing evangelism need to be highlighted. This is not an exhaustive list, but these strategies are the ones that I have found to be most helpful in reaching women for Christ with women in the local church.

MARKETPLACE EVANGELISM

> *Every day in the temple complex, and in various*
> *homes, they continued teaching and proclaiming the*
> *good news that the Messiah is Jesus (Acts 5:42).*

The first on our list is marketplace evangelism. We can see by the verse above, Acts 5:42, that part of the early church strategy was that they went daily to the temple complex and to homes. Their strategy was to go to certain marketplaces where the people were. They went to the temple complex where people were gathering and possibly thinking about religious things. They also went to various homes and shared, taught, and proclaimed the good news about Christ. In Matthew 10:5–42, we see even more instructions that Jesus gives for proclaiming Christ to the world. Luke 10:1–20 tells that Jesus sent out 72 ahead of Him to prepare for His arrival. The Bible is full of numerous strategies for taking the gospel to the marketplace.

In our ministries to women, we plan to reach women by going into their homes and creatively being out in the marketplace so that we may proclaim the good news. Planned outreach and following up after events are important biblical strategies that we need to plan for and adopt.

INTENTIONAL EVANGELISM

> *But you will receive power when the Holy*
> *Spirit has come upon you, and you will be My*
> *witnesses in Jerusalem, in all Judea and Samaria,*
> *and to the ends of the earth (Acts 1:8).*

Intentional evangelism is another form or strategy for evangelism. Intentional evangelism is just that. It is intentionally getting involved with the lost in order to form bridges and relationships so that there will be an avenue to share Christ. Intentional evangelism can come in various settings, in large groups, or with individuals.

We train our women to get intentionally involved in the marketplace and community to get to know those who do not know Christ.

Some examples of intentional evangelism are gatherings that are planned with the intention of presenting the gospel such as outreach breakfasts, dinner meetings, special events, and the like. Planning parties for friends, neighbors, and work associates during special events or holidays also can make great opportunities to build bridges and share about the love of Christ. I like to call these "parties with a purpose." Women can take the birthday parties, Christmas parties, and other parties they have and turn them into intentional evangelism events just by adding a few things. Taking hobbies like scrapbooking, cooking, and even fitness and looking for ways to share Christ are other natural settings for women to get together, have fun, and share about the truth that Jesus offers.

SEEKER EVANGELISM

When Jesus turned and noticed them following Him, He asked them, "What are you looking for?" They said to Him, "Rabbi" (which means "Teacher"), "where are You staying?" "Come and you'll see," He replied. So they went and saw where He was staying, and they stayed with Him that day. It was about 10 in the morning (John 1:38–39).

One of the most effective but least used strategies of evangelism is seeker evangelism. Seekers can be defined as those people who have not come to personal faith in Christ but are walking in that direction. They tend to be interested in the things of God and want to learn about Him and His truth. They are seeking Christ. They may or may not be aware they are seekers, but they are open and interested. Their openness makes for fertile ground for studies and discussions as well as special groups that present Christian principles like parenting classes, time management classes, Christian movies, and so many more.

Women in the church should plan seeker studies in homes and workplaces to study the Bible and just simply explain it. These studies can be scheduled over meals or anytime when women can gather and have some of their questions answered. One of the simplest things to do is just to open one of the Gospels and begin teaching, making a point to explain the basics of what the Bible is saying and how it applies to us today. Sometimes these studies can be given creative titles and point toward topics that might create interest and draw women to come. Seeker studies can be used inside the walls of the church or outside them in the community. Both should be incorporated in the ministry to women.

RELATIONAL EVANGELISM

> *He first found his own brother Simon and told*
> *him, "We have found the Messiah!" (which*
> *means "Anointed One") (John 1:41).*

Generally, relational evangelism is taking the relationships you already have in your family, with your friends and work associates, with your neighbors and others, and looking for ways to take those relationships to the next step and intentionally share Christ. It can also be looking to develop relationships with others who need Christ as well. We typically think about relational evangelism or friendship evangelism as something that is done one-on-one. While this is something women do personally, it is also something that the ministry encourages and for which it plans. We should provide opportunities and events to which women may bring women. I am known for having friendship retreats where we encourage each woman to bring an unchurched friend. This provides an opportunity for everyone to bring someone and also provides a setting where it is natural to talk about the things of God and answer questions as they come up.

Spontaneous Evangelism

The Bible is full of what I like to call spontaneous evangelism. This is evangelism that is simply and hopefully led by the Holy Spirit. Every time we share Christ, it should be by the leading and the power of the Spirit, but spontaneous evangelism is that which is not preplanned. Paul is converted and commissioned in Acts 26:9–18. It was something that God planned and was not planned by men. When we see Jesus talk to Zacchaeus in Luke 19, that is a door that God opened. When Philip was on the road and the Spirit led him to go share with the Ethiopian eunuch (Acts 8:26–38) is another example. Sharing Jesus while on your way is the kind of lifestyle evangelism about which I am talking. As leaders, it is important to share these experiences and encourage our women to listen to the Holy Spirit and look for the doors that God opens.

Servant Evangelism

For even the Son of Man did not come
to be served, but to serve, and to give His
life—a ransom for many (Mark 10:45).

An easy form of evangelism for most women is servant evangelism. Servant evangelism involves serving others and sharing the good news as the Lord opens the doors to do so. Forms of servant evangelism number as many as the stars, but some include things like washing windows and cars, handing out water bottles, cleaning up streets and areas in the community, and building and repairing houses for those in need. For women, some of the most used methods are things like cooking a meal or taking a pie to someone with a need, babysitting for single moms, lending a helping hand to someone at a store with an armload of groceries and kids, and numerous other things. What makes these good works evangelistic is when they are presented with an evangelistic message. Women may get the opportunity to explain that Christ is the reason for the act of kindness. They can also offer a word of testimony about the love of Christ or a note with a Scripture verse and a prayer given with the service in the name of Jesus. Servant evangelism can be something that individual women do, or it can be something that is planned in which the whole ministry is involved. I encourage each Bible study or prayer group to take on an evangelism ministry project during the semester. Servant evangelism projects are great for groups to do together.

IN CONCLUSION

Whatever the method used, evangelism doesn't just happen. It needs to be planned. To have an evangelistic ministry to women and reach them for Christ takes prayer and commitment on the part of every leader. For evangelism training and resources, check out the reference list or contact www.namb.net/heartcall for more information.

QUESTIONS FOR DISCUSSION

1. How can we bring the concepts of evangelism and missions back together? What are the ways we can encourage our women to reach people with the gospel of Jesus Christ?
2. Look at each aspect of making your women's ministry evangelistic. How can you incorporate praying for women to be saved, modeling the message, enlisting women, training women, involving women, reaching women, celebrating the decisions, and supporting the church in our ministries?
3. There are numerous ways to plan strategically to reach women for Christ. How can we reach women through each of the strategy areas listed?

Chapter 8

NURTURE

Women in Their Faith

Terri Stovall

*The 11 disciples traveled to Galilee, to the mountain
where Jesus had directed them. When they saw Him, they
worshiped, but some doubted. Then Jesus came near and
said to them, "All authority has been given to Me in heaven
and on earth. Go, therefore, and make disciples of all
nations, baptizing them in the name of the Father and of
the Son and of the Holy Spirit, teaching them to observe
everything I have commanded you. And remember, I am
with you always, to the end of the age" (Matt 28:16–20).*

We are gathered together, all except one. Some are
sure that he was the cause of it all, even if Jesus
had told us this would happen. If Judas had just not
betrayed Him, things would be different. Oh well, it didn't matter
now. We saw Him die that horrible death. We saw the body being
placed in the tomb.

The Sabbath was quiet after they sealed His tomb, each of us trying to answer so many questions in our hearts and minds. What would we do now? Had our trust been misplaced? Was He really the Messiah? He just had to be. The transformation in my life . . . in all our lives . . . was too significant. But now He's gone.

The women say that He's alive! How could it be? Peter didn't believe them and ran to check. It was true. His body was gone. The Jewish leaders and the soldiers are already claiming that one of us took His body. We just want some answers. So we are all gathered together, waiting . . . watching . . . wondering.

There He is. It's Jesus. He is here with us and He is alive! I immediately fall and worship Him in spite of my questions and doubts. Then He begins to speak. I can barely breathe. I sense it is our moment of truth. Will we, this small band of men, hear the heart of Jesus and have our lives set on a path that could change the world?

THE COMMAND

The narrative above could have been recounted by any of the 11 disciples who were present after the resurrection. It is the precursor to one of the more familiar verses in the New Testament related to evangelism and discipleship, the passage commonly known as The Great Commission (Matt 28:18–20). Jesus had much to say in a very short time. He did not try to comfort or apologize. In fact, Mark reports that He was somewhat irritated at the unbelief He found in His disciples (Mark 16:14). Jesus simply gave them their marching orders. In three short sentences Jesus answered the why, what, when, where, how, and who of the rest of their lives. Jesus' command that day to His 11 disciples is a command to every follower of Christ since then. Make disciples!

THE WHY: ALL AUTHORITY . . . THEREFORE

Jesus begins with a simple statement that reverberates throughout eternity. "All authority has been given to Me in heaven and on earth." Plain and simple, the *why* of everything that we do as believers in Christ is the fact that Jesus possesses the authority. I have heard many fathers answer the protests of their children with the statement, "Because I said so" or "Because I am the dad." A dad possesses a certain authority over his children. Similarly, we are God's children, and Jesus possesses authority over us. He holds authority not only on this earth but also in heaven. He has an all-encompassing authority that gives Him the right to say, "This is what you are going to do." It is neither our decision, nor is it under our own authority that we obey the commands of God. Note the connective "therefore" in verse 18 that unequivocally connects what was just said with what is about to be said. Why do we do it? Because Jesus said so.

THE WHAT: MAKE DISCIPLES

Now that Jesus has established who has the authority, He tells them what to do. Many may go straight to the word *go* as the command in this passage. However the only true imperative is "make disciples." The word *go* in the original Greek does have an imperative sense, but it is not a true imperative. It basically answers more the question of *when* rather than the *what*. The command in this verse is found in the Greek word that is translated "make disciples." Everything we do in this world as a follower of Christ is a response to the command to make disciples. Whether an evangelistic event, a Bible study, a women's retreat, a ministry opportunity, or a ladies' night out, everything should in some way have a role in making disciples.

THE WHEN: GO

Though not a temporal term, the word *go* in essence answers the *when* question. The action of this participle is coordinate with the main verb, the imperative "make disciples."[1] "Going" must occur before "making disciples" can take place. Jesus expected His disciples to be already among the people. A true disciple of Christ has no option but to go; one has to "go" in order to "make disciples." And truly, a woman who goes has the opportunity to make disciples. Some

---

[1] See the discussion of attendant circumstance participles by Daniel B. Wallace, *Greek Grammar Beyond the Basics: An Exegetical Syntax of the New Testament* (Grand Rapids: Zondervan, 1996), 640–45.

may say that they are not called to go but instead will pray for and support those who are out in the world making disciples. There is no exception clause here. A follower and disciple of Christ will go into the world for the purpose of making disciples. Going to all nations is not just traveling to another state or country or people group. This action intentionally engages the people one comes in contact with in order to share the message of Christ. It includes things like walking next door to visit a neighbor, sitting in a bleacher with mothers cheering on their children, speaking to the checker at the grocery store, or simply sitting on the edge of your daughter's bed talking through the events of the day. It involves crossing cultural boundaries, traveling to distant places, and seeing people as God sees them. Making disciples occurs when we intentionally engage others in this world.

THE WHERE: ALL NATIONS

Where is the Christian to go and make disciples? Again, a simple, all encompassing answer—"all nations." Christ came for all people of all time. While this may seem to be a given, remember the culture of the day. The Greek word used here could be translated as either "nations" or "Gentiles." While it is correct to translate it as "nations" here, it is important not to overlook what Jesus was saying. The predominant belief of the day was that the Messiah was going to come for the Jews first and only. Jesus had already shown by example that He came for everyone through His interactions with non-Jews, outcasts, women, and children. This statement removed any doubt that He was the Messiah for all people; "all nations" means *all* nations. Regardless of race, color, religious belief, physical location, or gender, Jesus came, died on the cross, and rose again that all may find salvation and a relationship with Him.

THE HOW: BAPTIZING AND TEACHING THEM

There are two steps to making disciples: baptizing and teaching. The follower of Christ is to lead people to faith in Christ and to disciple them in the faith. Too many times churches and ministries view evangelism and discipleship as mutually exclusive. Evangelism is the first step to becoming a disciple. If we focus solely on discipleship without the evangelism, then we are not truly making disciples. Evangelism is part of the disciple-making process and should flow naturally from the life of a disciple. Conversely, if we focus solely on leading people to Christ and do not teach them His ways, we may find ourselves surrounded by baby Christians who do not know how to walk in His ways. Paul warned of this in his letter to the Corinthians. "Brothers, I was not able to speak to you as spiritual people but as people of the flesh, as babies in Christ. I fed you milk, not solid food, because you were not yet able to receive it. In fact, you are still not able, because you are still fleshly" (1 Cor 3:1–3). We are commanded to present everyone mature in Christ (Col 1:28). God may very well hold us accountable for the lives baptized but not taught as well as the lives taught who never learned to become disciple makers themselves.

THE CURRICULUM: ALL THAT I HAVE COMMANDED

Christ gave specific instruction with regard to what was to be taught: "all that I have commanded." He does not say to teach the parts that relate to the culture of the day. He does not say to pick and choose what looks and feels good. He does not say to teach only that which matches our experiences or that with which we agree. Jesus says, "Teaching them to obey all that I have commanded you." Obedience to all that God commands is the mark of a true disciple. We are to teach the full counsel of God. We are to teach the easy, the hard, the basic, the deep, and even those things that are still difficult to grasp. We do not have the right to say, "That does not apply today." Remember the example of Christ. He reintroduced a God culture into a culture drifting away from Him. The way to do that is to teach *all* that He has commanded.

THE PARTNERSHIP: LO, I AM WITH YOU ALWAYS

Jesus concludes with a reminder of who is involved in this undertaking. His disciples are commanded to make disciples, but they are not doing it on their own. Jesus starts with a focus on His authority; in the middle He pauses to remind them that people are baptized "in the name of the Father and of the Son and of the Holy Spirit." He concludes with a word of assurance that He is with them always. The disciples have just seen their Messiah whom they thought they had lost and probably fear that He is leaving again. But even though Jesus left them physically soon after, they remembered that He would be with them, even to the end of the age. The word translated "end" paints a picture of completion until the time when all on this earth has been completed. That is a huge, overwhelming task that is not accomplished on their power. Paul wrote, "I labor for this, striving with His strength that works powerfully in me" (Col 1:29). Christ's disciples are in partnership with the one true living God, striving to accomplish God's mission through His authority and power.

THE COMMAND TODAY: MAKE DISCIPLES

Jesus' command to His disciples applies to every follower of Christ today including women. We make disciples through the power and authority of Jesus Christ. Women's ministries are to be going into the world, winning women to Christ, and teaching them the commands of God. Women's ministries are to teach the full counsel of God, helping women understand how to live as women of God in a twenty-first-century world. Women's ministries and their leaders do all of this in partnership with the one true living God, who is with them always, even to the completion of the age.

THE GOAL

In his letter to the Philippians, Paul wrote that his personal life goal is to "know Him and the power of His resurrection and the fellowship of His sufferings, being conformed to His death" (Phil 3:10). Paul also wrote, "We proclaim Him, warning and teaching everyone with all wisdom, so that we may present everyone mature in Christ" (Col 1:28). The goal is maturity in Christ—Christlikeness. Nurturing women in their faith is not simply deciding which discipleship course to offer but helping women know Christ and be conformed to His likeness. Jesus challenged Phillip by pointing out that they had been together for some time and Phillip still did not really know Him (John 14:9). Many women have taken every Bible study offered, attended every retreat and ladies' night out scheduled, but still do not comprehend the length, width, height, and depth of God's love.

It is easy to use words that we hear regularly in the church but not really know what they mean. In a recent seminary class, I asked the students to define *disciple* and *discipleship*. The first one they defined with some ease. A disciple is one who follows, learns, and emulates another. The word *discipleship* provided a little bit of a challenge. The suffix *–ship* indicates possessing character, quality, or behavior. So the term *discipleship* means to possess the character, quality, or behavior of a disciple. While our goal is to make disciples, many times we fall into the trap that our goal is discipleship. A better understanding is that as we are engaged in the activity of being a disciple of Christ, we are making disciples. Discipleship is more than the Bible studies, classes, and service opportunities we offer. These are the activities of being and becoming a disciple. Discipleship is the activity of our lives that reflects the one whom we follow, Jesus Christ. A fully developed follower of Christ possesses the character, quality, and behavior of Jesus.

For women's ministry we have chosen to use the term *nurture* rather than *discipleship* because it seems to convey what happens in woman-to-woman ministry better. In the same manner that a mother nurtures her child, woman-to-woman ministry is the older nurturing the younger to grow into a mature believer who then begins to nurture her own babes in Christ. The term conveys a sense of feeding, protecting, supporting, and encouraging. The goal of nurturing women in their faith is to see them to the point of being a disciple who emulates Christ and all that encompasses.

THE PROCESS

Disciple-making involves growth and is therefore a process. It is not checking the boxes as each stage is completed but a continual process of growth. Physically we do not grow in clear steps. Children do not grow from being three feet tall one day to being four feet tall the next day, even though they may seem like they do. We can stare at a plant and not see its shoots growing taller, but time-lapsed photography records the continual growth process. Growth in Christ occurs the same way. Completing a course does not ensure that growth has occurred. Conversely, the fact that someone has not been in a women's Bible study does not indicate a lack of growth. I cannot say this enough. Discipleship, making disciples, is not just about the studies we offer. It is about walking with women through life, feeding, protecting, encouraging, and supporting them as they come to know Christ all the more. While there are no magic formulas or programs that ensure spiritual growth, there is an organizing principle that helps keep us on track.

The women's ministry's discipleship program should be intentional. Intentionality is more than just selecting the latest Bible study or doing a leadership retreat because we always do a leadership retreat. There is an organizing principle that affects teaching and causes planning to take place. Adapted from Leroy Ford's curriculum design model, the graphic on the next page can help a women's ministry be intentional about nurturing women in their faith.[2]

SOMEBODY

The person that we are nurturing in the faith is the starting point to being intentional. The women that God has given us have unique yet similar needs. It is important to ask yourself several questions. First, how would you describe the women in your ministry today? Consider ages, family situations, work situations, and lifestyles, as well as common stresses, concerns, or issues. Second, how would you

---

[2] L. Ford, *A Curriculum Design Manual for Theological Education* (Nashville: Broadman, 1991), 55.

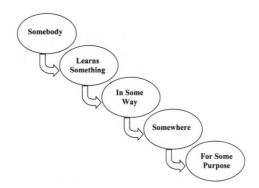

Diagram 8–1: Organizing Principle for Intentionality

describe the spiritual needs of the women in your ministry today? Determine whether you have women who are new to faith in Christ or new to the church, women who are growing, women who are stalled in their growth, or women who are ready for leadership. Last, what challenges are you facing in helping the women grow in their faith? Look at what is working and what is not. Identify any barriers to growth with which you are dealing. This can begin to paint a picture of "somebody" who needs to be nurtured in her faith.

LEARNS SOMETHING

Jesus told us to teach everything that He has commanded. A women's ministry's discipleship program should be comprehensive. That is, it is to teach the full counsel of God. The Bible is the curriculum to teach, and the goal is to abide in Christ; we do that by teaching women to live by God's Word, to pray in faith, and to witness to a lost world. It is helping them learn how to build godly relationships and how to minister to others. It involves helping a woman grow in faith spiritually, mentally, emotionally, and physically.

We know the body of material to teach; the intentionality comes in knowing what to teach when and to whom. When I served as minister to women, my secretary was a fairly new Christian and a practicing Catholic. Having never been a part of a women's Bible study, she wanted to take part in one of the fall studies. One of the studies that fall was a rather in-depth study, and I knew that if she tried that study, she would have struggled. She needed something that introduced her to Bible study other than the in-depth study that was geared toward more mature believers. It was a good move. Today she has grown to the point that she is leading ministries in her own church, but it was a process of growth. At the same time I had women who were ready to dive into the deeper studies of Scripture, and we provided opportunities for them. My leadership team wanted training on how to lead and to understand who they were as leaders, and we did that. Today several on that leadership team are leading women's ministries in various churches. The important thing was not to look at the opportunities as choosing the latest and greatest or to provide a cafeteria where one could pick and choose from seemingly unrelated items but that it was an intentional process. Everything that is offered, planned, and scheduled should have a specific woman and goal in mind.

In Some Way

There are all different kinds of ways to learn. Individually each woman has a different predominant learning style. Some learn best by listening (auditory learners), others learn best by seeing (visual learners), and still others learn best by moving (kinesthetic learners). We tend to teach and lead out of our own preferred style of learning, but that is not always the best way to help a woman learn and grow. Sitting and listening or sitting and watching are good, but there is so much more that we can do. The point to remember here is to understand your women and to offer a balance of listening, seeing, and doing.

Connection and relationship are also important to women. That is one of the reasons we have found that the typical evangelism training models generally do not appeal to women. Women do not want to learn an outline to which they have to remain faithful. They would rather learn what Scriptures to go to, such as the "Roman Road" passages (Rom 6:23; 3:23; 5:8; 10:9–10) and then interweave their own testimony with the plan of salvation. Women who are lost are not so interested in the bullet points of an outline but want to know what difference Christ has made in your life. When looking at curriculum resources and ways to help women grow in their faith, consider how women communicate and learn. We want to give women the opportunity to hear biblical truth and then be able to discuss its application in small group. We do so not as an opportunity to ask, "What does this mean to you?" but rather, "How will you apply this truth to your life?"

The growth of women's Bible studies has brought a vast array of Bible study options. The video-driven Bible studies (where a video of the primary teaching is played to the large group and then the group divides into smaller groups to discuss the lesson) have grown in popularity because of their ease of use and sense of quality teaching. While this may give the perception of growing women in their faith, the best discipleship occurs in small groups, taught by a live teacher who builds relationships with the women. Remember the mandate of Titus 2. The older women are to teach the younger women how to be women of God in this life. The relationship between the older and the younger is just as much a part of teaching process as is the content. A teacher on a video does not know what a young viewer is dealing with and cannot answer her questions directly. A teacher in a large group cannot know every need that is present in that large group. Women today are craving for connection with real women who are grounded in truth to teach them how to walk in the truth. The task of nurturing is not just sitting and listening. It is engaging with one another for growth.

SOMEWHERE

The task of nurturing a woman in her faith can occur anytime, anywhere. Do not get stuck in the box of thinking that it is primarily happening in the Bible study group that meets at the church on Tuesday evenings. Consider the possibility of offering a Bible study in a home, where women are taught God's Word while experiencing the ministry of hospitality. A woman can continue the growth process as she serves alongside another woman, preparing meals for the women's shelter. A leader can hone her leadership skills by leading a subcommittee for a special event. Disciple-making can occur at church, at home, in small groups or in large groups, one-on-one, and everything in between. Let's take this back to our organizing principle for intentionality. After considering who is learning, what she is going to learn, and how she will be taught, then consider the best place.

FOR SOME PURPOSE

Everything we do is to nurture women in their faith so that they will become more Christlike. That is the purpose. For intentionality, it is necessary to break that down into a smaller bite. The purpose may be that a new believer learns the basic disciplines of the faith. The purpose may be that a group of preschool moms understand and apply biblical principles in mothering. The purpose may be to develop a new group of leaders. The purpose is the anchor that holds it all in place. Sometimes we may work through each of the circles and get to the last one and realize that the way we are teaching does not match the purpose. Maybe the content is good, solid content, but it is really the wrong thing to teach right now because it does not help us accomplish the purpose.

PUTTING IT ALL TOGETHER

Now that we have gone through each part, let's see how this all fits together (see table, next page).

SOMEBODY	LEARNS SOMETHING	IN SOME WAY	SOMEWHERE	FOR SOME PURPOSE
Preschool moms	Biblical and practical parenting	Mentoring relationships	Quarterly meetings at church plus mentoring times	To give new moms a foundation for parenting
New to the faith	Disciplines and distinctives of the faith	A new believer's class for women	Home group that meets for 10 weeks	To know and understand what it means to follow Christ
Growing believer	In-depth Bible study on Philippians	Bible study group taught by one of our teachers	At the church when child care is available	To understand the joy that comes from a life with Christ
Leadership development	How to do a particular aspect of the spring retreat	Shadowing or apprenticing with a current leader	The spring women's retreat	To develop future leaders

Do you see how this helps to keep everything intentional? Once you start with the somebody and begin to see that woman as God sees her, the other parts will begin to fall into place. Somebody learns something in some way, somewhere for some purpose.

TIPS FOR NURTURING WOMEN IN THEIR FAITH

Every women's ministry will structure its disciple-making ministry differently depending on whom they have to disciple. There is no right or wrong way to do it, as long as you are helping women to grow in Christlikeness. There are several tips, however, that can help as you plan for the year's activities and events.

PEOPLE FIRST, PROGRAMS SECOND

Ministry is about the people. Leadership is about the people. Programs are tools to be used to reach and nurture the people, not to dictate the direction of a ministry. We can learn a lot from the way other churches carry out their ministries, but do not sacrifice the work God is doing with your women for the sake of a program. It is OK to offer the latest Bible study if it helps your women grow in Christ. It is also OK to do something else if that is what your women need to become more Christlike. It is about the people, not about the programs.

KEEP CHRIST AND THE BIBLE CENTRAL

Christ is the focus of who we are and what we do. We live in a culture that screams, "It's all about me!" when really it is all about Christ. Once again we are reintroducing a God culture into a culture that puts God in the second seat. It is so easy to focus on what the women want, what makes them feel good, and what they can get out of it. In reality, it is continually pointing people back to Christ and what He receives from us, not the other way around.

The Bible is His message to us and the center of all we teach. Many good books have been written by men and women of God that offer great insight into life, faith, relationships, and even Scripture. Yet the Bible is to be our primary textbook. The Bible gives God's standard on life, faith, relationships, and even Scripture. "For the word of God is living and effective and sharper than any two-edged sword, penetrating as far as to divide soul, spirit, joints, and marrow; it is a judge of the ideas and thoughts of the heart" (Heb 4:12). No best seller written by man can even come close to that.

FOCUS ON TRUTH NOT EXPERIENCE

Today's postmodern world interprets truth through experience. Some question whether there is such a thing as absolute truth. John proclaims the fact that Jesus is truth over and over again in his Gospel (John 1:14,17; 8:44; 14:6,17; 17:17). Too many have fallen into the trap of interpreting Scripture through experience as opposed to interpreting experience through Scripture. Focus on truth not experience. Rather than asking, "What do you think this means?" or "How does this make your feel?" ask, "This is what God's Word says; how do we apply this to our lives today?" God's Word does not change with the seasons or with the whims and emotions of women. God's Word remains the same today, yesterday, and tomorrow. It is truth. We have the task of helping women know, understand, and embrace truth.

EXPECT GROWTH AND MATURITY

Expect the women to grow and mature. In joint partnership with God, He will cause the growth. We do not cause the growth to happen as echoed in Paul's words to the Corinthian church: "I planted, Apollos watered, but God gave the growth" (1 Cor 3:6). But we should not be surprised by the growth. If we expect the growth, we will do all we can to make sure the conditions are right for growth. Whether it is time to plant or water or pull weeds, we work the field to allow God to mature women in the faith.

EVEN TO THE END OF THE AGE

The command of Christ to make disciples was not just to the Eleven gathered together that day. He promises to be with us "even to the end of the age," until all has been completed. We will not reach that day of completion until Jesus Christ comes again and we meet Him face-to-face. Until then followers of Christ are to continue to walk the path that Jesus mapped out to the eleven disciples. We are to make disciples by reaching women for Christ and nurturing them in the faith, through the authority and power of Jesus Christ until the time is completed.

QUESTIONS FOR DISCUSSION

1. Identify a group of women in your ministry. Working through the organizing principle presented in the chapter, how will you nurture these women in their faith?
2. Which of the tips for nurturing women is the most difficult to follow, and what are some safeguards that can be put into place?
3. How can a women's ministry make sure they keep Christ and the Bible central?

Chapter 9

INVOLVE

Women in Kingdom Work

Terri Stovall

*Now there are different gifts, but the same Spirit. There
are different ministries, but the same Lord. And there are
different activities, but the same God is active in everyone
and everything. A manifestation of the Spirit is given to each
person to produce what is beneficial (1 Cor 12:4–7).*

*E*very Christmas it is a tradition in my family to break out
a large jigsaw puzzle that the entire family will work on
throughout the holidays. Probably the least enjoyable part
of this tradition is taking out all the pieces and separating the border
pieces from the rest of the puzzle. Every piece must be picked up
and examined to see if one of its sides has a straight edge. If it does,
it is a border piece and goes on the table. If it doesn't, it goes back
in the box. The shape of the piece determines where it fits in the
puzzle. Some pieces look so much alike that their shapes are almost
identical. That's when you begin to look at the color of the piece

trying to match it to the picture on the box. Sometimes, as the puzzle progresses, you can stand and try 20 different pieces in one spot before you find the one that fits perfectly. And when all the pieces are perfectly connected and no piece has been lost or forgotten, a beautiful picture is completed.

The task of involving women in kingdom work is much like solving a jigsaw puzzle. It is a time-consuming job of examining the shape of each woman and trying to find just the right spot that she fits so that when everyone is exactly where they are supposed to be and no one has been forgotten, a beautiful picture of God's church at work is created.

BIBLICAL FOUNDATION

In the classic *Celebration of Discipline*, Richard Foster writes, "As the cross is the sign of submission, so the towel is the sign of service."[1] If a follower of Christ cannot take up the towel and wash feet, then she should not be called a follower of Christ. Those who are growing and maturing into Christlikeness will find themselves yearning for opportunities to express the servant nature of God that grows within. We do not have a choice but to serve.

We have been created to serve. "For we are His creation—created in Christ Jesus for good works, which God prepared ahead of time so that we should walk in them" (Eph 2:10). Not only were we created to serve, but we were saved and called to serve. Paul writes to Timothy that Christ "has saved us and called us with a holy calling, not according to our works, but according to His own purpose and grace, which was given to us in Christ Jesus before time began" (2 Tim 1:9). It is in the DNA of our nature to serve. As one grows in her walk with Christ and becomes more like Christ, she will be drawn to service. It is what we have been created, saved, and called to do.

We have been gifted to serve. God does not call His people to service and leave them wanting. Every believer has been gifted for

---

[1] R. Foster, *Celebration of Discipline* (New York: HarperCollins, 1988), 126.

the service she is to fulfill. In Romans 12 and again in 1 Corinthians 12, Paul is clear that we are all gifted, each with her own gifts in order to work together for God's kingdom. Peter writes, "Based on the gift they have received, everyone should use it to serve others, as good managers of the varied grace of God" (1 Pet 4:10). The purpose of the gifts received is not for our own benefit but to serve others. Paul reiterates this specifically in his letter to the Ephesians that the purpose of the various gifts is that the body of Christ will be built up. To possess a gift and not use it in service to others or to use it for our personal gain goes against God's purpose for the body of Christ. God has given every believer His gifts to serve the body of Christ and to bring glory to Him.

We have been commanded to serve. Paul writes in the letter to the Corinthians that we have been given the ministry of reconciliation and that we are Christ's ambassadors. Being an ambassador carries with it the connotation that we not only represent Christ, but we go with a message and a mission. Our mission is to be a people with a ministry of reconciliation (2 Cor 5:16–21) that is best carried out by emulating the life of service that Christ modeled. In the midst of a squabble over who is greatest, Jesus reminds His disciples that it is the one who serves that will be greatest and a true disciple acts from a heart and attitude like His—one who came to serve and to give his life for many (Matt 20:20–28). To answer the call as a Christ-follower is not to wear a crown and seek recognition but to pick up a towel and wash the feet of a people who need to be loved.

A life of service is a natural response to a personal relationship with Jesus Christ. We are a people who have been created to serve, and when we accept the gift of salvation that Christ offers, we are called to a life of service by the very nature of Christ. God gives us the resources to serve this world and His church through His authority, His power, and through the unique gifts that He bestows upon us. It is not a choice to serve. We serve out of obedience to His command but ultimately out of His love for us and our love for others. In the process of becoming a mature disciple, sometimes the desire to serve is greater than the ability to find a place to serve.

Women struggle to know where and how to become involved. At this point the women's ministry and its leaders can partner with a growing believer to find the best way to be involved in the work of the kingdom.

THE ROLE OF THE WOMEN'S MINISTRY LEADER

The role of the women's ministry and its leaders is critical to helping women become involved in kingdom work. The leadership sets the tone for service. Ministries see more women answer the call to service when they expect women to become involved, provide the tools and resources to help them find their place, and offer opportunities for service. A women's ministry in a large metropolitan church was trying to determine its role in a church whose goal was that every member would serve somewhere. The women's ministry came to the realization that helping women find a place of service was not about places of service in the women's ministry. The best role for the women's ministry was to help a woman find just the right place that matched her giftedness, ability, and passion, even if it was in other church or church-supported ministries. They quickly became a resource point for funneling new leaders and volunteers to ministries throughout the church, and women found just the right fit for them.

One of the elements to making disciples is to help women find their place of service and to fulfill the servant nature of Christ. Blanchard and Miller offer an acronym for "serve" that reminds the leader of important principles of leading others to service.

> **S**ee the future.
> **E**ngage and develop others.
> **R**einvent continuously.
> **V**alue results and relationships.
> **E**mbody the values.[2]

---

[2] K. Blanchard and M. Miller, *The Secret: What Great Leaders Know and Do* (San Francisco: Berrett-Koehler, 2007), 95.

These five principles remind leaders that they are always to look ahead to what they need and opportunities that may arise in light of the vision God has given. Leaders are constantly to be engaging others to help them grow and develop the skills and gifts God has given them. Leaders are never satisfied with the status quo but are constantly looking for new ways to accomplish goals and tasks. A leader has a balance of focus on the task at hand and the people involved. One does not supersede the other; they go hand in hand. Finally, the leader embodies the values of the ministry and the call. A leader who wants her women to be involved in service as the natural outflow of faith in Christ should also be involved in service reflecting her relationship with Christ.

The role of the leader is critical to involving women in ministry and kingdom work. If it is not important to the leader, it will not be important to those whom she is leading.

HELPING WOMEN FIND THEIR PLACE

Involving women in ministry requires intentionality, just as it did in reaching women for Christ and nurturing women in their faith. For many women it is not an easy task to find a place of service. When I left my position on church staff in order to join the faculty at Southwestern Seminary, I thought that it would be fairly easy to find a place of service. It was much harder than I expected. Even though I was comfortable around the church, knew the people and the staff, it was difficult actually to find a place to serve. I can only imagine that if I, who had grown up in the church and am very comfortable there, had trouble finding a place, how much harder it must be for someone who does not have the same church background. We need to make it easy for women to try out and find just the right place for them.

A PUZZLE PIECE

The first step is to help a woman understand her gifts, talents, skills, and experiences that shape who she is. Similar to a jigsaw puzzle, each piece has a certain shape that determines where the piece fits. Before we start trying to plug that piece into the puzzle, we need to see what it looks like. There are many different programs available that help guide a person to understanding her best fit for ministry, but they all essentially look at the same things: spiritual gifts, skills, passion, and experience.

Spiritual Gifts. Every believer has been given one or more spiritual gifts. Scripture is clear on that. Surprisingly many women do not believe that they have any gift, much less a spiritual gift. Helping a woman discover and understand her unique gifting is the first step for many women to realize that they can be used by God. Spiritual gifts are a good place to start, but they are only a part of what shapes a woman for service.

Skills and Talents. As we go through life, we learn skills, and natural talents and abilities are honed. Identifying those things that a woman does well matched with a spiritual gift can begin to help a woman see how she can be used in ministry. We possess hundreds of skills and talents. The key here is to identify those things that we do well and enjoy doing. Begin by asking what she likes to do at home or for what she is known. If she works outside the home, find out what job skills she uses. Ask her if she has ever been told she has a natural talent for something. These questions can help a woman identify the unique abilities she has.

Passion. When we talk about passion, we are talking about the one thing that gets us excited and motivated. It is the thing that we will choose to do above all others if given the choice. This question may not be as easy a question to answer. Some women may not have found their passion. Others may still be discovering it. When a woman identifies her heart passion, she can begin to identify the venue within which she will use her gifts and skills.

Experiences. Living life brings with it a myriad of experiences. Some are normal life-development experiences such as singleness, marriage, parenting, and widowhood. Life can also bring painful experiences such as the loss of a child or abuse. God comforts and strengthens us in our afflictions so that we may in turn strengthen and comfort others who are afflicted. Paul used the challenges and sufferings that he faced for the cause of Christ by not counting himself a victim but rather recognizing God's comfort, provision, and deliverance. He then was able to help others who might be going through similar tribulations (2 Cor 1:3–7). While the women in your church may not face the same persecutions Paul endured, God can use a woman's experiences, the painful, the spiritual, the normal life experiences of this world, to serve others who may be going through something similar. For women who have had devastatingly painful events in their lives, the final step of healing often comes when they are able to use that experience for good in someone else's life.

Women have been shaped by the gifts they receive, the skills and talents they possess, the passion that gets their hearts racing, and the experiences of their lives. To help a woman find her best place of service begins with helping a woman understand. Women can serve in the short term just about anywhere. But the longevity of service and the growth that comes from serving are best found when she finds just the right place.

PLACEMENT

As the women's ministry leader, you have just taken a woman through a spiritual gifts inventory, helped her identify her abilities and her passions and know about her life experiences. Now what? This is where a lot of women's ministries and churches stall. Churches will have an emphasis on spiritual gifts and take an entire congregation through the identification process and then not do anything with it. Just because we have helped a woman understand how she has been shaped for ministry, our job is not complete. The next step is to help her find the best fit. Even though a puzzle piece can be forced into the puzzle, the best place is where its shape naturally fits.

The role of the leaders at this juncture is to know what opportunities are available and the best fit for that area of service. Then we can give women options. Similar to a jigsaw puzzle where we try a number of pieces before finding just the right piece that fits, women should be given the opportunity to try a place of service before giving a long-term commitment. Some churches have gone so far as to offer "first-serve" opportunities where people can try a place of service or shadow someone for a month or a couple of weeks to see if it is what they expected. As much as we can try to determine what the best match might be, it is not until we try it that we see whether it is really a good fit.

The importance of a good fit and good match cannot be overemphasized. When a person finds just the right place, then that person will tend to remain in service longer, be more invested in that place of service, and develop faster as a leader than when the fit is a little off. It is difficult to describe, but if one has been on the hunt for just the right place to invest her life and then finds it, she will know it and so will you.

Give Them What They Need

Once a person has been placed, we need to give them what they need to have the best possible opportunity to succeed in this area of service. God gives us the resources we need to do what He has called us to do, and we should do the same. It is the tendency of the church to enlist people to places of service that can have eternal ramifications on the lives of others and never give them the training or resources needed to do the job well. The first step to helping them succeed is to offer some kind of orientation. Orientation gives an overall picture of what is happening in this area of service and what role that person will play.

The second step to helping one succeed in an area of service is to offer training. Initial training helps a person get off to a good start, but ongoing training helps a person grow and mature in the area of service. Training in the midst of serving is just as much a part of discipleship as is Bible study. Once again you will hear the word *intentional* as training should intentionally address the needs of the one serving along with the mission and vision of the ministry. It helps bring purpose and meaning to the training being offered.

The last step is to provide the resources needed. Resources can come in the form of curriculum, space, equipment, money, or people. When we involve women in the work of the church, we do not want to leave them without the necessary resources to do what they have been called to do and we have asked them to do.

FOLLOW-UP AND REDIRECTION

Your job as a leader is not yet complete. Whether you have enlisted someone to serve in the women's ministry with you or you have helped to facilitate the placement of a volunteer in another ministry, it is important to follow up with her. Sometimes we finally get someone enlisted and a vacancy filled, and we are immediately off to the next one, and that person never really hears from us again. Be sure to go back and check with her. Find out how it is going and if she still feels that this is where God wants her to be. Following up with her will send the message that you are still interested in her and what she is doing. It will also give you good feedback on the ministry and areas of service in which she is serving. Sometimes it will give her the opportunity to tell you that this is not really what she had in mind. When that happens, then it is time to redirect her to another place of service.

There is a place of service for everyone in the body of Christ. For some it takes time to find just the right place. As a leader, you have made the commitment to involve women in service and in kingdom work. If one place does not work, then find another place for her to serve. If that does not work, then go to the next. The one thing that we do not want to do is to convey the message that there is no place for you. Everyone has a place of service in the body of Christ.

A HARD PIECE TO PLACE

Suzanne was always the first to volunteer. She wanted to be a part of everything. Her enthusiastic attitude would help us overlook the rough edges and awkwardness that made finding a permanent place of service difficult. When I mentioned in passing that I was looking for a new Sunday school teacher, she immediately volunteered, but that was really not the place for her. She was involved in some way with every committee that helped plan the retreat. Some of that went well; others just chalked it up to, "Well, that's just Suzanne." I soon found myself with the attitude of just putting up with Suzanne and giving her things to do to placate her.

One day Suzanne stopped by my office. Her exuberance was not quite there that day. In fact, she was as solemn as I had ever seen her. When we sat down together, she took a deep breath and told me through tear-filled eyes that she loved her church and just wanted to find something that she could do. She wanted to find her place. We talked a long time that day, and for the first time I saw Suzanne as the woman God had created her to be. A woman who loved Jesus, she was growing in Him and was willing to give everything she had to be used by Him.

Over the next few months, I worked with Suzanne individually. We spent time looking at spiritual gifts and helping her understand the responsibility of using those gifts. We talked through the different skills she had and helped her realize that even those things that seemed to be everyday abilities for her were skills that could be used in the church. The most meaningful time spent was talking through her life experiences and how God could use those experiences for others. It was touching to see a woman talk about the hard road she had walked and the differences with which she lived. She grew in the process to realize that these things were not deficiencies but weaknesses through which God could work.

Then we began to try different places of service. We tried all different kinds of things, but nothing just seemed right. Watching her try different places of service, I began to see a trend. Her favorite thing to do was to talk to people, give them a smile, and always say something positive. I soon came up with an idea. Suzanne became our official women's Bible study greeter. It was her job to be at the women's Bible study 15 minutes early and to make sure everyone who came was greeted with a smile and a positive word of encouragement.

Suzanne thrived in that role. It gave her a sense of purpose. The women in the Bible study began to see Suzanne as an important part of the Bible study experience. On the rare occasion when she was absent, she was sorely missed, and many made sure Suzanne knew that. Today Suzanne is a different person. She still has her unique differences, but she has matured and grown through this place of service as only Suzanne can. Everyone has a place of service in God's kingdom. Some pieces are easy to identify where they fit. Others are more difficult. As leaders of women, we have the responsibility to help every woman find just the right place to use her gifts for her King.

QUESTIONS FOR DISCUSSION

1. If you had to describe your theology of service, how would you define it and support it with Scripture?
2. What is the role of the leader in service and involving others in service?
3. How can women's ministry help a woman discover and understand her spiritual gifts?
4. Have you ever had a hard piece to fit such as Suzanne? How did you help that person find her place?

Chapter 10

ENGAGE
the Next Generation

Jaye Martin

*Timothy, my child, I am giving you this instruction in keeping
with the prophecies previously made about you, so that by
them you may strongly engage in battle, having faith and
a good conscience. Some have rejected these and have
suffered the shipwreck of their faith (1 Tim 1:18–19).*

*H*er name was Mrs. Bowers, and I will never forget her.
When I was a young teen, she sat with my friends and
me every Wednesday night at church. She pulled out
her Bible, and she taught us; she loved us, prayed for us; and she
answered our questions. Every week we would bring friends from
school along with our questions about girlfriend issues, boy issues,
and life issues. Mrs. Bowers would write down the questions and
bring us back the biblical answers the next week. She always acted
as if she needed to research and find the answers for us, but looking back on it, I think she knew we'd be back the next week for the

answers. She didn't have to wear the trendy clothes, and I certainly don't remember whether her nails were done or not; but, when I think about ministering to the next generation, I cannot think of a better example than Mrs. Bowers.

ENGAGING THE NEXT GENERATION

Regardless of how old we are, there is always a generation right behind us. We just need to open our eyes to see who they are and train the younger women to be the godly leaders for their generation and for the next one. We must engage these women in such a way that they will be ready to engage in the battles that are to come. In Deuteronomy 20:2–4 we read,

> *When you are about to engage in battle, the priest is*
> *to come forward and address the army. He is to say to*
> *them: "Listen, Israel: Today you are about to engage*
> *in battle with your enemies. Do not be fainthearted. Do*
> *not be afraid, alarmed, or terrified because of them.*
> *For the LORD your God is the One who goes with you to*
> *fight for you against your enemies to give you victory."*

We must train the young women that God will be with them, fight their battles for them, and lead them to be victorious in their Christian walks.

The next generation of women leaders will come from the girls we grow up today. In the abnormal culture we live in, we must focus our attention on these incredible young women and give them the tools they need to lead the next generation.

WHY A MINISTRY TO GIRLS?

> *In the same way, older women are to be reverent in*
> *behavior, not slanderers, not addicted to much wine.*
> *They are to teach what is good, so that they may*
> *encourage the young women to love their husbands*
> *and children, to be sensible, pure, good homemakers,*

and submissive to their husbands, so that God's
message will not be slandered (Titus 2:3–5).

It doesn't take a lot of insight to know why we need a ministry to girls. Take a gander at the magazine stand the next time you check out of the grocery store. It is filled with the promises of a world gone south, and I don't mean to the Caribbean. Open your e-mail, and chances are that even with the filters on, horrific e-mails have wormed their way into your inbox. Turn on the television set, and you will see commercials for things at which our mothers and fathers would blush. A trip to the mall will shock you with the window displays. Even from the safest sites on the Internet, we can be drawn away from the godly to the down-under with one fatal click. It takes a lifetime to grow up a child in the way she should go, and yet one image will continue to return again and again when imbedded in the mind. I don't think I need to give any more specifics to the ways of the enemy here, but there is plenty of evidence why we need a ministry to girls.

BIBLICAL PHILOSOPHY FOR MINISTERING TO GIRLS

Love the LORD your God with all your heart, with all
your soul, and with all your strength. These words
that I am giving you today are to be in your heart.
Repeat them to your children. Talk about them when
you sit in your house and when you walk along the
road, when you lie down and when you get up. Bind
them as a sign on your hand and let them be a symbol
on your forehead. Write them on the doorposts of
your house and on your gates (Deut 6:5–9).

While the words in Deuteronomy were written about teaching our children, they can also be applied to teaching the next generation of girls. Certainly, our children are our first priority, but there is much room for us to mentor the next generation of young women in the ways of the Lord. The Scripture is clear: loving the Lord is the beginning. When we allow Him to be in our hearts and lives, we have something to say to others. We have something to tell them. We don't need to know every subject or have all the answers; we just have to know to go to Him and to His Word and direct these young girls to put Him first. As reminders, we are to talk about the Lord constantly—when we sit at home or walk along the road, when we lie down and when we get up. We bind these Scriptures on our hands and live in such a way that everyone will know that we are His. We put them on our refrigerators, and the dashes of our cars, and on our bathroom mirrors. When we love the Lord with all our heart, souls, and strength, we have something to pass down to those who follow.

Everyone doesn't have godly parents. It would be nice if they did. Because of this, it is essential that we become role models for the girls who need to see what a godly woman looks like—in the flesh. You see, just to know that we are to live a godly life is not enough; we must show young women what it looks like to dress appropriately, to live the life of a Christian woman who is a daughter, mom, friend, grandmom, and the rest. When girls don't see this at home, they don't always understand the application. Just as God sent Jesus to show us what it means to be a Christian on earth, He sent women to show young girls what it looks like to be a child of the King.

I remember a young graduate student who came to seminary fresh out of college. She had found the Lord recently and was doing all she could to grow in the Lord as fast as she could. She shared with me that no one in her family was a believer and that she had only been around a few Christians. She was passionate about girls' ministry because she could have benefited from some wise counsel during her formative years. Even at the time she was sharing how she had benefited by just hanging out with me. Things she picked up on were not the big things; they were the little things like how to respond to those who served us coffee, how to get in and out of a car (appropriate for a woman), and other seemingly insignificant issues. These were things that I would have never thought to teach her, yet they were things that helped her to live out what she had read in the Scriptures but had not seen lived out. The need for godly women to be with young women is a real need for ministry.

PURPOSE OF GIRLS' MINISTRY

The reason for girls' ministry is simple; it is similar to the purpose of ministry to women. The purpose of ministry to girls is to reach girls for Christ, nurture them in the faith, involve them in servant ministry, and support the youth ministry and church. These tasks of girls' ministry support the very function of the church that is evangelism, discipleship, ministry, worship, and fellowship. How girls live out their lives every day is how they worship God. There is corporate worship when the church comes together to worship God and hear the proclamation of His Word. So, while we may worship together with girls, this is not the purpose of the ministry. How we worship is how we live out evangelism, discipleship, and ministry in our ministry to girls. This is why we reach girls for Christ, nurture them in the faith through discipleship, and help them to serve in ministry appropriate for young women.

Fellowship flows out of working together in reaching, nurturing, and serving. Therefore, it is important to understand that the purpose of girls' ministry should not be just for fellowship. To focus only on girls getting together leads to fat Christians and models that girls just need to have fun. The real fun is helping young women understand that leading girls to Christ can be the most exhilarating high that they could ever know. The real fun is growing that new believer into a godly young woman who can stand up for Christ in her home and at her school. The real fun is seeing that growing young believer become involved in servant ministry in her church and in the community. When we reach girls for Christ, grow them up in the faith, and help them get involved in the lives of others, we can know that they will be plugged into the fellowship of the girls' ministry, youth ministry, and the life of the church for years to come.

BEING THE LEADER THAT GOD INTENDED YOU TO BE

Chances are we have all heard the saying: "Everything rises and falls on leadership." Who knows who said it first? I have read it in many leadership books, and I believe it. Leadership makes the difference. For the next generation to be great leaders, we must be great leaders ourselves. Those who follow us will do what we do. I remember one of my bosses who went to meet with one of the great leaders of the faith. When asked what the secret to great parenting was, this leader said that the secret was to be a great person. Kids do what their parents do. Parents can teach kids to act in such a way that is different from how the parents are living, but generally children do what their parents do. It is essential that we *be* the leaders that God calls us to be so the generation behind us will be ready to take up the mantle and be the godly women leaders that God calls them to be.

Ask any young girl about when her youth leaders are authentic, and she will tell you just who is being consistent in their walk and who is not. Young people can see straight through us. They can see the inconsistencies. They instinctively know whether we are living lives of integrity. Being a godly leader is important, but being a godly leader with young girls is essential. I know of a young woman leader who was serving with girls in her church. It turned out that this leader had some of her romantic interludes posted on one of the popular connection Web sites. Another leader found her out, fortunately, before the young girls found her. What was she thinking—that she could hide on the World Wide Web? We must watch what we say and do out in public and behind closed doors because young girls are watching—needless to mention the reminder that God is watching. I use this rule of thumb for myself: if I cannot talk about it or feel the need to cover whatever I am doing with anyone, then I should not be doing it. Think about that for a minute. We must continue to analyze and take before the Father every part of our lives, not only because of our relationship to the Lord but because the lives of young women are at stake.

Enlisting Leaders

Being a godly leader is essential for us who work with girls. Enlisting godly young girls to work with us is our next area of business. When working with girls, it is important to give everyone the opportunity to feel like a part of the team. Some might say that only a few need to lead, and I would argue that it is crucial that every girl be given the opportunity to learn to work with the team and to lead. There may be degrees of leadership, and no doubt some will rise to the top and be able to take on more responsibility, but the purpose of the girls' ministry is to grow them up to be godly young women and to lead others to be godly young women. Therefore, we must help all of these girls learn to take on responsibility and to be a part of what God is doing in the life of the youth ministry and the life of the church.

As a young married adult without a child, I was the outreach leader for the youth ministry at my megachurch. The youth ministry was incredible, and the new youth minister was building a great discipleship ministry with these young people. There were thousands of youth on the church roll. There was no system in the ministry for youth reaching other youth. All of it was dependent upon adults reaching them. While there was certainly a need for an abundance of adults to be involved, there was also a need for the youth to be organized to reach other youth. I was able to set up a system to have the youth volunteer to be care group leaders. These youth leaders were given four or five youth in their class to call and with whom to keep in contact. They were also the ones that were given the challenge to reach out to others and to call those who visited the class or our special events. It was amazing to see how these young leaders rose to the challenge. Not only were we reaching youth, but we were helping to train these young people how to carry on conversations with others and to develop healthy relationships. To this very day I still am in contact with many of these who are now godly leaders in their homes and in the church.

When my daughter was entering high school, it was my joy to be asked to serve with a mother-daughter charity league that was forming in my neighborhood. I must admit that I spent years downplaying charity groups because I felt they were just doing social ministry and had missed the point of Christ-centered ministry. While I still prefer to serve through the local church, this became a growing point for me. I realized that it was an awesome opportunity to share the love of Christ with those in the group as well as those to whom we ministered. This group asked me to be the vice president who would oversee the grade-level groups of girls. The girls were middle school and high school aged girls; and since I had worked with youth for years alongside my husband and been a Girl Scout leader, I seemed like the obvious choice. As I saw that each grade level would have about 25–30 girls, it became a challenge to see how we could involve each girl in some sort of leadership position. In order to be fair and keep the same girls from always being the president, I wrote all the positions on cards and had the girls draw one. Each had a job and went to training where moms helped them to know how to do that job. The next year the names went into the basket again, and everyone had a different job. Some of the natural leaders, who had always gotten all the attention, learned to serve in different ways. Some who never would have thought about being a leader ended up with jobs that had more visibility. It was an incredible time of learning, and it was great to see the girls rise to the challenge. I was able to teach them the principles of biblical leadership and show them how these leadership truths flowed out of who God is—His character. If we can do this in a secular group, then certainly there is more reason to do it in the local church. Whether we involve some or all the girls, we must grow them up to lead like godly women.

BUILDING TEAMS

One of the aspects of growing young leaders is helping these leaders work together in teams. Girls are naturally relational. They love to work and play together. In fact, they like to do just about everything together. Building teams usually comes easy. Working in teams can lead us back to knowing that it is easier to do it ourselves. Helping girls work as a team is part of growing girls to lead. God gives each of us gifts and talents to be used in ministry in the church. As we help these young girls learn to discover their leadership strengths and weaknesses, we also help them learn to work with the strengths and weaknesses of others. Teams can be a fun way to reach other girls for Christ, grow girls in discipleship, and do ministry projects together. We are also able to help the girls learn how we work as a team with the youth ministry and the church. Team ministry is crucial in the ministry to girls.

Tasks of Girls' Ministry

Reach Girls for Christ

> *Then Jesus came near and said to them, "All authority has been given to Me in heaven and on earth. Go, therefore, and make disciples of all nations, baptizing them in the name of the Father and of the Son and of the Holy Spirit, teaching them to observe everything I have commanded you. And remember, I am with you always, to the end of the age" (Matt 28:18–20).*

As we develop our ministry to girls, reaching girls for Christ is critical. I have watched girls' ministry spring up in the last few years, and I am thrilled that as a body women are seeing this need and desiring to disciple the girls in their youth groups. However, I am continually devastated when I hear how many of these ministries do not include outreach. How can we leave out the rest of the Great Commission? Matthew 28:18–20 is clear that we are to go, make disciples, baptize, and teach. While the local church is the one to do the baptizing, we must go and share Christ with the girls in our communities. We must mobilize our girls to reach those girls who live in the community and who go to school with them. We must help them cross cultures and lead girls to Christ. We must take them on mission trips to the downtown areas, to the suburbs, across the county lines, around the country, and to the ends of the world if we want to show them what evangelism and missions are all about. When girls are given the opportunity to do evangelism and missions, they usually grow up to be mission-minded young women with hearts for the world.

Reaching girls for Christ is not just about having pink brochures and salon parties. We want to help girls understand that our self-esteem comes from the Lord. Girls will come if there are caring, loving women who are willing to listen and help them grow. While the color pink can be a part of what we are doing and may attract a few, this generation is out to change the world. They are excited about multicolored, multicultured ministry and as a whole are drawn more to serving and even saving the world. Reaching girls today means that we give them opportunities to get out there and serve in the community and around the world. If we think we are reaching this generation of girls with pink alone, then we had better rethink things.

You have heard it before: evangelism is caught rather than taught. Girls want to be outreach oriented when they see that we are reaching people with the gospel of Jesus Christ. Of all the people whom I have known in evangelism, let me tell you about one of the most effective—if not *the* most effective—that I have even seen, especially with girls. Her name is Gay. Gay was an incredible young woman. She was married with a young son when her husband was killed in a plane crash. Gay taught me how to reach girls. Gay taught in our eleventh-grade Bible study department. Before the class even started, she contacted every girl in her class. One by one, she went to a see a girl and talked to her about accepting the forgiveness that Jesus offered through His death on the cross and about making Him the Lord of her life. Then she asked which of their friends needed to know Jesus. She took that girl and went to the friend's house. Within a few short months, Gay's class went from about 10 to about 25 girls. There were numbers of baptisms, and it started a movement in our whole department. Lives of workers and youth were changed as we saw the simple truth of proclaiming the gospel of Jesus Christ in such a simple way. Gay loved these girls and she loved Jesus. She loved Him enough to make sure they all knew one another. Reaching girls for Christ will be caught when we decide that we love Jesus and love girls enough to introduce them.

Nurture Them in the Faith

He established a testimony in Jacob and set up
a law in Israel, which He commanded our fathers to
teach to their children so that a future generation—
children yet to be born—might know. They were
to rise and tell their children so that they might
put their confidence in God and not forget God's works,
but keep His commandments (Ps 78:5–7).

After we reach girls for Christ, discipleship is essential. We must walk these girls through the basic principles of prayer, meditation, Scripture memory, Bible study, sharing their faith, and all the wonderful truths involved with being a child of the King. We must take the time to nurture them in the faith.

I want to tell you about a 16-year-old named Sharie. I met her when the mom who adopted her as a baby brought her to a discipleship meeting on a Thursday night before the Friday discipleship weekend started. Sharie had tried to commit suicide on Wednesday night, and her mom turned to our church for help. There they both stood, looking at me, begging for help. The mom was desperate; Sharie looked scared to death. She was a tall, beautiful girl without a single flaw showing. We shared a few minutes, hugged, and I assured them both that the weekend would be a great way to get involved and back on the right track. I have no doubt that I pulled off a confident and loving appearance, but I went home and fell on my face before the Lord wondering what on earth I could offer and what would happen if she tried it again while she was with us. The weekend went incredibly well. Sharie accepted Jesus as her Savior that weekend, and God worked in incredible ways to restore her life. The church youth reached out to her, and a tall young boy fell head over heels for her—which, as you know, goes with the territory of working with young people. Over the next months and years, I came to know Sharie quite well. She went on to finish high school, graduate college with a degree in accounting, and marry that godly young man who believed in her. Today she is a mom of two young boys and has faithfully served the Lord in her home and by working with other young children. Oh, how good God is! Oh, the benefits of reaching girls for Christ and growing them up in the faith.

Nurturing girls is more than just telling them a Bible story. Nurturing girls in discipleship is helping them see, learn, and study what it means to be a Christ follower. It is all about helping them discover these truths and apply them one at a time. It is about using the Bible as our text and not relying on all the outside books. We can use other studies from trusted writers and publishers, but we must keep the focus on *the* Book. There is great power in reading the Word of God individually. There is great power when the Word of God is read aloud. As we use resources, it is crucial that we make sure they are resources that focus on the Word, help us understand it, and help us apply it. Nurturing girls in the faith depends on getting girls into the Bible.

INVOLVE THEM IN SERVANT MINISTRY

> *Based on the gift they have received, everyone*
> *should use it to serve others, as good managers*
> *of the varied grace of God. If anyone speaks, his*
> *speech should be like the oracles of God; if anyone*
> *serves, his service should be from the strength God*
> *provides, so that in everything God may be glorified*
> *through Jesus Christ. To Him belong the glory and*
> *the power forever and ever. Amen (1 Pet 4:10–11).*

We have already touched on this: girls love and need to be involved in ministry. It is great to involve as many girls as possible in leadership and team opportunities but also in serving opportunities using their spiritual gifts and talents. Young people are gifted in so many areas, and often it takes so much time to help them that it seems easier to do it ourselves.

Each girl comes with a unique combination of spiritual gifts and talents. Look for ways that girls can be involved. I have allowed so many young girls to give a minute devotional, read Scripture, organize a trip to see a girl who needs encouragement, share the plan of salvation, and many more things. We can bring a few girls with us as we take food to a family in need, make outreach visits, and attend church meetings and services. As we go, we are able to get to know the girls more personally and see the ways that we can plug them into service. With students we especially need to be careful not to overwhelm them with long-term jobs. While there may be some jobs that last the school year, there should be many little jobs so they can serve. The one who uses her talents to sing or play the piano might be enlisted to lead the music one week rather than enlisting her to lead it every week. Girls who are overwhelmed tend to drop out because they do not always have the confidence to know they can do it. Several girls who are gifted in administration or like to plan parties might be encouraged to help you plan the class party or the next girls' event. These girls are ready to serve with their spiritual gifts and talents, and we need to create the opportunities for them to do so.

Involving girls in service is more than just serving in the class or girls' ministry. Any way we can involve them in reaching, discipling, training, leading, and serving is wonderful for growing girls to lead in the future.

SUPPORT THE YOUTH MINISTRY AND THE CHURCH

Therefore, we ought to support such men, so that
we can be co-workers with the truth (3 John 8).

Love for the local body of believers, the church, is something that we must teach the girls whom we reach, nurture, and involve in servant ministry. Christ died for the church. We are to die to ourselves for the cause of Christ. We are to train the next generation to support the local church and to love her with our hearts, souls, and minds. There is no perfect body of believers, but when we come together as the local church, we become the body of Christ in a lost world. As we serve together, we show the world what Jesus did. Girls love to support a cause, and there is no cause greater than the cause of the local church.

We support the church by supporting the pastor, staff, and youth ministry leaders and by serving under their authority. We are not here to do our own thing or create a ministry to girls apart from the local church; we are here to involve girls in the ministry of the church and to help them learn to love the local church and to represent her in every way. Young women can be a tremendous help with children and preschool activities. They can be helpful in serving and church-wide fellowship activities. They can be instrumental in encouraging the pastor, youth ministry leaders, and members by being involved in worship services. They can be positive role models to the younger girls. They can be encouragers of the elderly women. The ways to support the ministry of the church are numerous.

MINISTERING TO GIRLS FOR THE LONG HAUL

In conclusion, as we minister to girls, we always want to keep in mind that we must minister for the long haul. Gone are the days when flashy events were all that were needed in ministry. Big events will always draw the girls, and we can continue to have these as our time and budgets allow, but ministry to girls is an ongoing project, and it is much more than creating a big event. It is a day-in and day-out, long-term project. So remember not to start at a pace that cannot be continued. Many fail in ministry because they burn themselves out, and girls' ministry is one of the easiest ways for burnout to take place. Burnout happens when our output doesn't keep up with our input. What I am saying is that you must spend time with God and allow Him to pour Himself into you. Ministry to girls and women is simply an overflow of our passion for the Lord. When we start doing the ministry ourselves rather than depending on God, then burnout is usually right around the corner. Our lives need to be balanced not only between the time we put into girls' ministry and our personal lives but balanced spiritually as well.

As we look at starting or tweaking a ministry to girls, it is important to remember that everything we do in the local church should be done in conjunction with the pastor and the youth ministry leaders. Our attempts to come alongside them may be misunderstood if we have not done the spiritual preparation needed in advance. If you are seeing the need for girls' ministry, let the youth minister give you direction on how you can be involved and help. We always want to make sure that we are under his leadership. Pray and ask God for His timing and allow Him to open the doors. He wants girls ministered to more than we do.

QUESTIONS FOR DISCUSSION

1. Find passages in the Bible that would support your having a ministry to girls. Discuss these as a group and make a list of the main ones.
2. What other reasons, besides the biblical ones, would there be to have a ministry to girls?
3. If you wanted to approach the pastor or youth ministry leader about helping to get a girls' ministry started, what would you say? Prepare a list and discuss what and how this might be done.
4. Discuss each task of girls' ministry and how you would lead girls to do these areas.
5. Talk about the ways you might find women to lead in this area of ministry. How would you determine if they were the kind of leaders that you wanted?

Chapter 11

SUPPORT
the Church Family

Jaye Martin

*Many women who had followed Jesus from
Galilee and ministered to Him were there,
looking on from a distance (Matt 27:55).*

*And every day they devoted themselves to meeting together in
the temple complex, and broke bread from house to house. They
ate their food with gladness and simplicity of heart, praising
God and having favor with all the people. And every day the
Lord added to them those who were being saved (Acts 2:46–47).*

*I*t was time for the annual Christmas pageant, and we needed
some people who would serve as hostesses and be in charge of
a booth to provide information about our church. The women
of the church stepped up to serve. There was a need for Sunday
morning extended session workers (those who could keep the babies
and preschoolers during the worship service). The women of the
church stepped up to serve. Vacation Bible School needed more

workers. The women of the church stepped up to serve. There was a need for women to tutor children in an after-school program at a nearby apartment complex. The women of the church stepped up to serve. On Saturday mornings some were needed to help with our mission churches. The women of the church stepped up to serve. There was a family who had visited the church who lost a child, and the family was in need. The women of the church stepped up to serve. Do you get the picture? Women are to support the work of the church. No matter what the need, we are to be there to serve the church and through the church serve the world on behalf of Christ. What would churches do without women who have a passion for the body of believers that we call the local church?

In a day when so many have decided that we do not need the church, we must continue to rally our women to step up to the plate and to serve and support the church body. We have already looked at how important it is to involve women in ministry, but supporting the church goes beyond that. Supporting the church means that we don't do *our* ministry; we do the ministry of the church. When the pastor has a vision to reach those in the apartments around the corner, women should be the first to step up and support him. When the church decides that they need to raise money for new ministries, women need to be there to lend their help and support as well as all their resources. Women are a huge part of the local church, and we are not there to do our own thing or our own little ministry. Yes, we are to minister to women, but we are also there to minister to the body and to support the needs of the church. We are not there to be the pastor to women and run our own congregation; we are there to support the ministries that are already taking place. We are there to fill in the gaps and to support the church as a whole.

I know of several couples who are church starters. These godly couples would never conceive that there should be a men's ministry, children's ministry, or even a youth ministry—much less a women's ministry. The group is small and they are all involved. With the body of Christ, they do not separate by age and gender; they are one body. Even as they grow, they do the work of the church—together. This is not to say that there is not a place for ministry to those in these areas, but it is to say that support of the overall church comes before the specific needs of any group.

Even in a large church, when the ministerial staff determines that during the week of Easter the whole church will focus on a week of outreach to the community, then there is no place for the women to gripe because they want to have a spring fashion show the week before. The men would never decide that their annual barbeque took greater importance. The children's ministry hopefully would not think that a Saturday Easter egg hunt would be more important than preparing for Easter services. The point is, women are an essential part of the church, and they are the church organized to do the work of the church. There will be times when it is appropriate for the women to have separate studies and training. Likewise, there are times when they need to rise up and fill the need of the church at large. Imagine the pastor's face when a woman leader offers to help him carry out God's vision of evangelism, discipleship, and ministry. Support for the local church is the joy and privilege of every woman and every person in the body.

BIBLICAL FOUNDATION

For as the body is one and has many parts, and all the parts of that body, though many, are one body—so also is Christ. For we were all baptized by one Spirit into one body—whether Jews or Greeks, whether slaves or free—and we were all made to drink of one Spirit. So the body is not one part but many. If the foot should say, "Because I'm not a hand, I don't belong to the body," in spite of this it still belongs to the body. And if the ear should say, "Because I'm not an eye, I don't belong to the body," in spite of this it still belongs to the body. If the whole body were an eye, where would the hearing be? If the whole were an ear, where would be the sense of smell? But now God has placed the

*parts, each one of them, in the body just as He wanted.
And if they were all the same part, where would the
body be? Now there are many parts, yet one body.*

*So the eye cannot say to the hand, "I don't need you!"
nor again the head to the feet, "I don't need you!" On the
contrary, all the more, those parts of the body that seem
to be weaker are necessary. And those parts of the body
that we think to be less honorable, we clothe these with
greater honor, and our unpresentable parts have a better
presentation. But our presentable parts have no need of
clothing. Instead, God has put the body together, giving
greater honor to the less honorable, so that there would be
no division in the body, but that the members would have
the same concern for each other. So if one member suffers,
all the members suffer with it; if one member is honored,
all the members rejoice with it (1 Cor 12:12–26).*

The biblical foundation for supporting the local church can be seen throughout Scripture but is most readily seen in 1 Corinthians 12:12–26. This is the passage on the body of Christ. Christ is the head, and we are all parts of the body of Christ. This is a picture of the universal church but also a picture of the local church family of believers. Each believer belongs to the body. Each is uniquely gifted for ministry in the body of Christ. No one or part is unimportant. Even those parts that seem hidden are essential. Each person and area are part of the whole. When one is missing, the rest suffer. What an incredible picture of how we are to support the church! Each woman is important, and her contribution is vital to the church.

We must come back to this biblical foundation as we think about the ways and reasons to support the church. While we are to be Titus 2 women and reach, teach, involve women in ministry, and engage the next generation, we are to support the church. We are part of the church as a whole. To remove the women is to remove the very heart of the church. As leaders, it is imperative that we live out and model what it means to support the church family.

SUPPORT THE PASTOR

One of the joys of supporting the church is the joy of supporting the pastor. There are numerous ways to support the pastor. One of the first ways is simply to support him verbally. We can look for ways to encourage him, but we can also stand up for him when we hear people being critical. We should never serve "fried pastor" for Sunday lunch. Our pastors have a hard enough job without the criticism that comes with the territory. Too many believe that they are helping by showing the pastor where he needs to improve or what he needs to do, and this could not be farther from the truth. If we discern a problem, it is a call to prayer. It is not our job to call the pastor on things; it is the job of the governing body if there is a real problem rather than a perceived one.

Another way to support the pastor is to support the things on which the pastor focuses. If the pastor emphasizes the need for the church to come together and serve the community on a certain Saturday, the way we support him is to be there with as many as we can bring with us. If the pastor shares the need to park across the street so the visitors can have a close place to park, then we should look for ways to support him in this effort if at all possible. We may not be able to support the pastor in every single thing, but we can support him as he leads. Even pastors understand the seasons of a woman's life, and they understand that our homes, husband, and families often stand in the way of supporting certain events and extras.

Supporting the pastor can also come in the form of supporting his wife and family. Often the pastor's wife feels great pressure to be a certain way or to be involved and there every time the church doors are open. Looking for ways to relieve her pressure is a wonderful way to support the pastor. It might be something like allowing her to come or not come to the women's events, asking her to be the advisor rather than the director of something, helping her by allowing her to drop in on a Bible study rather than being there for the whole morning or evening. Every pastor's wife will come with a unique set of gifts and talents. She needs to be supported whether she is directly involved in the ministry to women or not. Ultimately, she is serving by taking care of her husband and children. Her season of life, as well as her giftedness and talents, will determine a lot about where she will be able to be involved. She may have a passion for the worship ministry or the children's ministry or some other area. Involve her to the extent that she wants to be involved and support her regardless of her level of involvement.

Another way to support the pastor and his family is by praying for them. We do not have to know the details of their lives to know that we can pray for God's protection for them, His vision, His provision, and the list goes on. When a need is shared or comes to light, it is important that the need be a matter of prayer. Prayer for the pastor does not mean that we tell others the need but that we take it to the Father in prayer and trust that He can handle it.

SUPPORT THE STAFF

Support for the staff of the church is another important way that we can lend support to the church. I have always been involved in churches that have multiple staff. The ways that we can support other staff members are numerous. Let me give you some examples. At my home church of Second Baptist in Houston, I try to support the staff by getting to know them and just being an encouragement. Often the support staff do major work without much notice or praise. These men and women of God work long hours and carry out the ministries of the church. They have a laundry list of things that have to be done in any given day. Since I served for years in a ministry position, I am aware that the pastor delegates many things for them to handle. Anytime I can help a staff member by handling a problem, carrying out an assignment, or just lending support, then that is something that I do. Sometimes it means that I do not look at them as people who can do things for me but as people for whom I can do things. While it is important to remember them during special holidays, it is also important to remember them on a regular basis.

162

Taking an interest in their families and their ministries and bringing honor to them is so important. Praying for them and asking for their requests is a meaningful ministry.

SUPPORT THE CHURCH FAMILY

Part of supporting the church is supporting the families of the church. Many times the deacons and Bible study groups take on the job of ministering to families in need, but the women's leaders should look to the pastor and staff for direction on how they can support the church family and families. This does not mean duplicating ministries that are already happening, but it can mean that we see the needs and help to fill in the gaps. Obviously before we start any area of ministry, we need to go to the pastor, staff, or leaders in charge of the ministry and share our willingness to be of help.

Support for the church family can come in many ways. It might mean that we see that there is a need for someone to help new parents or new moms by visiting just after the baby is born. There might be some personal or specific needs that the church staff is aware of where the women can help. Maybe a single mom wants to attend a Bible study, and child care is not available during that study. A lady who could volunteer to help with the child and do homework can be a great support to the family and the church.

SUPPORT THE MINISTRIES OF THE CHURCH

In addition to supporting the families of the church, we also want to support the ministries of the church. When the Sunday morning Bible studies need teachers, we can look to the women's leaders to help fill the need, and we can even put them to work calling people that might be qualified to help teach or substitute. If the recreational programs need people to volunteer to be coaches, we may be able to help find some godly young dads who would be available to help. Let's say that there is a need to help serve a meal at the church during a fellowship. Surely the ministry to women could help to find someone to serve. There are so many ways to support the ministries of the church both individually and as a group. There is nothing more amazing at a church than for one ministry to serve another ministry, and yet this is what God calls us to do—to be servant leaders.

As I think about serving and supporting the ministries of the church, I remember with fondness the joy from serving the church community. It was fun to have the women's ministry leaders greeting during a church outreach event. It was a joy that we were able to decorate rooms so that other ministries could enjoy them. It was exciting to see how many women came to Christ because our women had visited them in their homes and shared the gospel of Jesus. We should support any ministry that we can. And the great thing is, while we do not do it for what we get, often these ministries will be the first to support us when the need is on our end.

We also support the ministries of the church by the calendar. We are careful not to schedule over things that other ministries are doing. Our church calendars are usually overloaded with all kinds of things so it can be difficult to plan, but we must be selective in what we schedule and when we schedule it. If the men want to host a baseball event the same weekend that the women want to hold their retreat, then we need to offer to go to another weekend—regardless of whether a certain speaker is available. We can share our concern, but if not heard, sometimes it is best to support the other ministry and lead our women to see the importance of doing so.

Support the Functions of the Church

The way we support the ministries of the church is important, but it is also important to support the ministry functions of the church. We are the church. We are the church organized to do evangelism, discipleship, ministry, worship, and fellowship.

Evangelism. The Bible does not say to go out two by two on Monday night. However, everyone is given the responsibility to share the good news. I know many people who feel that if the pastor is evangelistic and the church is reaching people, then they are off the hook. The Great Commission, however, is for everyone. We may prefer to share Christ through our relationships, creative parties, seeker studies, and serving acts, but we must be about the task of evangelism and supporting the outreach and evangelism ministries of our local church.

Discipleship. Whether we are involved in the women's ministry or not, we still need to be involved in the disciple-making process of the church. Discipleship is Bible study; it is church training; it is helping new believers know the spiritual disciplines of the faith; it is everything that is about being a Christian. To support the discipleship area of the church means that we are involved in these areas. Of course we cannot do everything, but we can support the main things. There are basic things such as being a part of the Bible study group of the church. I am a strong believer that women need to be trained by women and need times when they are together. I am also a strong believer that families need to be together. At my church all the Sunday morning Bible studies (or Saturday night, should one choose that option) are coed. Therefore, it would not be right for me to go just to women's studies and not go with my husband on Sunday mornings. Nor would it be right for him just to attend his early morning men's group and not be with me on Sunday mornings. Even when we are working in the children's, youth, or college area, we still must be involved in Bible study together. Families that stay together study the Word together. Supporting the discipleship ministries of our churches is essential.

Worship. Way too many women who are involved in speaking to and teaching women never find the time to be a part of the church in corporate worship. We are not to give up meeting and worshipping together. Scripture is clear. When we let our Bible study time keep us from attending church worship services, then we have done a disservice to the body. When we think that attending a Bible study with worship for women allows us to be absent from the church body worshipping together, then we have missed the point that God asked us to come together as a body and worship. There is no excuse for the women of the church to feel that they are exempt from church services. Being a part of the local church means that we are to give of our finances, resources, lives, and time. As leaders, we must be about public worship as well as private worship.

Ministry. Involvement in ministry is important on a personal level both within and outside the church. We are to use our gifts and be involved in ministry inside the church as well as in the community. We support the ministry of the church by being involved in ministries as a group of women leaders but also by being involved individually.

Fellowship. The fellowship in the book of Acts is the fellowship that flows out of serving together in the church. True fellowship happens when we serve the Lord together. No matter how close I am to women in my neighborhood, I am even closer to those with whom I have served in ministry. There is no greater fellowship than when we have worked for months on a study and see the joy that women experience when they understand what it means to be a Christ follower or when they come to know Jesus personally.

If you have ever gone on a mission trip, then you know that it can be so deep an experience that it is hard even to share what happened when you return. The bonding of fellowship can be so great that we cannot even express it, and it is a bond that lasts forever. I can tell you that some of the great things I have done in serving have given me the best fellowship that could be known to man. Those women who work hours on a retreat—who pray, prepare, study, toil, and labor—gain much fellowship far beyond those who just attend the meeting. To support the fellowship of the church, we are to be an integral part of it in every way.

Find the Need and Fill It

Supporting the church family also means that we find the need and fill it. When we see a need in the church, we should be part of the answer to that need. When there is a problem, we are to be the solution. If we show up to leave our child in a class and a worker is sick, we should be the first one to stay and help. When there is paper on the floor in the hallway, we should love our church enough to pick it up. When the copier is stuck, we should try to fix it.

I do not have the gift of service. On every spiritual gift inventory I have ever taken, service is not something in which I score more than a point, if that. Yet I have the mandatory command in Scripture that I am to be a servant. That means that I am to support my church in every way. As a leader, I must serve. I must be the first one to set up the chairs, make the copies, go find the pencils, sharpen them, and hand them out. I need to make the coffee when it is empty. I need to do what needs to be done.

As leaders of women, we must model servanthood. We must model what it looks like to see the need and fill it. I am appalled at so many women leaders and speakers who think they have arrived and are above this. They expect others to serve their needs and wait on them. I allow men to open the door for me—in fact, I love it— but when one is not around, I jump to serve by opening the door for those with me. I am amazed at how many don't even offer to get the door. I am surprised at how many times I will call a church or Christian institution and am passed from person to person because no one stops to say, "Let me find the answer for you." I am saddened when I see Christian women, and especially leaders, walk right by and not offer to help someone who obviously needs help. Find the need at the church and fill it. We are to serve others and to support others. Whatever the need is, especially at church, we need to quit looking for someone else to fill it and jump to meet the need for the cause of Christ.

BIRTH NEW MINISTRIES

It seems obvious to me that women are the ones who birth things. We birth babies for sure, but we also birth new ministries. Who better than women to start a new ministry that is needed, grow it up, and send it out to be a part of the overall church?

A lady in our ministry saw the need for the young moms to know how to parent. She started a study on this, and it changed lives. The dads wanted to come, and she knew it would change the dynamics of the group so we went to the discipleship pastor, and he took it under his wing. He enlisted this lady's husband and other couples to serve in this ministry. I loved the fact that we had birthed a parenting ministry and loved just being a part of it. When we birth new ministries and grow them up, we have to be willing to let go of them. They are no longer under our wing but someone else's. It doesn't take away from the ministry to women; it adds to it. There were now young moms and dads learning to be godly parents.

Birthing new ministries can go both ways. When I began to serve in women's ministry, there was a retreat ministry that was under the activities ministry of the church. The minister in charge had seen the need and enlisted women to coordinate and put on this huge retreat. When the staff made my job into a full-time job, the retreat then came under my leadership. Even though the activities ministry had started it, they were happy to include it in its proper area with the rest of the ministries for women.

In Conclusion

We have barely scratched the surface in ways that women can support the church family. What a joy it is not to be a separate ministry but to be part of the body of Christ in every conceivable way. We consider it an honor to contribute to the church family by constantly looking for ways to be supportive.

Questions for Discussion

1. List the ways your ministry to women could support the pastor, other staff, and their families.
2. What are the main ministry areas of your church? How can you lead women to support these areas, both individually and as a women's ministry?
3. Discuss how your women's team can be supportive of the functions of the church: worship, evangelism, discipleship, ministry, and fellowship.
4. What are some of the needs of the church that women might be able to help with and thereby support the church body?

5. Discuss ministries that your women's ministry might be able to start, grow, and then give for another area of the church to oversee. These might be things that take a lot of manpower to birth but, once established, would be easy to maintain. (Of course, we always get permission before starting any ministry.)

Part Four:
Women's Ministry in Praxis
How Do We Do It?

*"For I know the plans I have for you" —this is the Lord's
declaration—"plans for your welfare, not for disaster, to give
you a future and a hope. You will call to Me and come and pray
to Me, and I will listen to you. You will seek Me and find Me
when you search for Me with all your heart" (Jer 29:11–13).*

*W*hy do we lead women? In the first section we laid the biblical foundation upon which to build a women's ministry. Building upon that foundation, we then examined who we are to be as women leading women in the church. Then section 3 answered the question of what we are to do: we are to reach women for Christ, nurture them in the faith, involve them in ministry, engage the next generation, and support the church family. We are not to be the pastor to the women. The church already has a pastor. We are to mobilize women to complement the pastor by leading women to support the church. We support the church by helping her to reach women, disciple women, involve them in ministry, and grow girls to lead the next generation. Now we are ready for our last section. Section 4 answers the question, How are we to do it?

How are we to lead women to lead women? We begin with prayer. We look to the Father to show us through the Word. We look to Him for His vision. When we have it, we plan strategically. Unless we plan to do the ministry to women God's way, it will be easy to get off track. As we plan, we enlist our team. We look for women who are godly role models and exemplify Christ in every endeavor. We seek to change. We are in the business of changing hearts for Christ and helping women grow and changing what we are doing to align with the Word of God. As we change, there will be conflict, and we seek to handle these realities in a way that honors God. And how do we lead? We lead with excellence. We lead in such a way as to honor the King of kings. As daughters of the King, we can know that He will be honored with women leading women to serve Him with passion and purpose and under the awesome authority of the local church. To God be the glory for the things He will do.

Chapter 12

Strategic Planning

Terri Stovall

Catch the foxes for us—the little foxes that ruin the vineyards—for our vineyards are in bloom (Song 2:15).

Lord my God, You have done many things—Your wonderful works and Your plans for us; none can compare with You. If I were to report and speak of them, they are more than can be told (Ps 40:5).

The verse from Song of Solomon quoted above, believed to be spoken by the woman to her lover, is a reminder to the church that we who are in leadership have the responsibility to protect what has been entrusted to us. Like little foxes that enter a vineyard, eat its fruit, and trample down the growth, Satan's tendrils can creep in and begin to destroy the vineyard that we are tending and keeping watch over. These intruders can move us off course just enough that we soon find ourselves drifting far from God's plan for the ministry. What do they look like? They can come in the form of cultural pressure to do the latest thing whether it fits our ministry or not. Foxes can be in the shape of guest speakers whose theology contradicts the theological beliefs of the church, but they made us laugh and feel good. They come in the form of laissez-faire leaders or members who are never held accountable. They are cunning and enter through places we never imagined. More often than not, I have found that foxes can get in because no one is watching. No one planned for them.

A Biblical Basis for Strategic Planning

I have been asked on many occasions how much we should plan and how much we should just allow the Holy Spirit to lead us. The people asking this question seem to view planning and God as being mutually exclusive as opposed to being partners. God has given us our marching orders and our overall purpose, but God has also given each of us a brain, the ability to reason, and the ability to put feet to His plan for the Church. Scripture both illustrates and admonishes that we are actively to carry out the plans of God. If we don't, we leave our vineyards open to the little foxes.

Planning with Purpose and Order

Scripture abounds with examples of God's people partnering with God to carry out His plans. Moses is a clear example of an ordinary man doing extraordinary things for God. Many will go to the story of Jethro confronting Moses on his inability to delegate. I like to look earlier in his life. Can you imagine what kind of planning it took to get all of the children of Israel moving in the same direction at the same time when they left Egypt? That is more an illustration of being an extraordinary planner than the example of Jethro's confrontation. Moses knew the destination. He knew when it was time to move. He knew God was with him. But I am sure it took every ounce of his reason and meetings with Joshua, Aaron, and the tribal leaders literally to put feet to God's plan. Now that's what I call a planner (Exod 12).

What about Joshua? He is a vivid example of one who knew God's plan and how it was to be carried out. He did not waiver even if it did seem like a crazy way to take a city. After all, who marches around a city for seven days and then takes it down with a blast of trumpets (Josh 6:1–27)?

Nehemiah is the epitome of a planner and one who could make decisions, deal with the critics, the government, and the people all at once (Neh 1:1–11; 2; 4:1–6).

David is credited with putting together one of the greatest leadership teams known to man. He continually sought the Lord's direction for each step he led the people to take (2 Sam 2:1–4; 4:9–12; 5:17–25; 7:18–29).

Paul was intentional in carrying the gospel to people who had not heard. He was not one to close his eyes and throw a dart at a map to decide which town to travel to next. Paul was specific in the route that he took. With that said, he is also an example of one who was ready to make changes when God redirected his path (Acts 16:9–10).

While on earth Jesus showed Himself to be the ultimate planner. He came for a purpose and with a plan and did not allow anything or anyone to steer Him away from that plan. He did nothing haphazardly or without intention. Every word, every step, every act, even the ultimate act of sacrifice was carried out to fulfill the plan of the Father (John 6:38). When the religious leaders challenged Him on the plan that He was fulfilling, He was steadfast and clear on the direction He was walking (Luke 5:30–32). He stayed in constant contact with the Father who sent Him (Matt 14:23; Luke 9:28; 11:1), and when He knew the steps ahead were going to be painful, He once again went to the one who sent Him (Matt 26:36–46). Then He finished the plan set before Him.

ADMONITION FROM THE PROVERBS

God not only gives us examples of people who carried out His plan with purpose and order, He also admonishes us to be intentional about planning. The book of Proverbs overflows with such admonitions.

- "The inexperienced believe anything, but the sensible watch their steps" (Prov 14:15).
- "Plans fail when there is no counsel, but with many advisors they succeed" (Prov 15:22).
- "The lot is cast into the lap, but its every decision is from the LORD" (Prov 16:33).
- "A man's heart plans his way, but the LORD determines his steps" (Prov 16:9).
- "Finalize plans through counsel, and wage war with sound guidance" (Prov 20:18).
- "Commit your activities to the LORD and your plans will be achieved" (Prov 16:3).
- "The plans of the diligent certainly lead to profit, but anyone who is reckless only becomes poor" (Prov 21:5).

It is clear just from this small sample that God expects us to be about planning. God expects to be a part of that process, but He also wants us to do our part. Scripture reminds us that we are to be sensible, seek counsel, allow God to determine the steps, and always be diligent.

What exactly is meant by *planning* and more specifically *strategic planning?* I say *strategic* planning because the mission God has given us is so critical that it must be a plan that takes into account as many variables, conditions, and opportunities as possible while never wavering from the ultimate objective.

As I tried to settle on one definition of strategic planning that can be applied to the ministry of the church, I discovered that this is not a cut-and-dried task. Many definitions have been given and restated.

- The process of thinking and acting[1]
- A disciplined effort to produce fundamental decisions and actions that shape and guide what an organization is, what it does, and why it does it, with a focus on the future[2]

---

[1] A. Malphurs, *Advanced Strategic Planning: A New Model for Church and Ministry Leaders* (Boston: Baker, 2005), 11.

[2] J. M. Bryson, *Strategic Planning for Public and Nonprofit Organizations* (San Francisco: Jossey-Bass, 1995), 4–5.

• A multifaceted plan designed to reach an objective[3]

Webster's dictionary does not define *strategic planning* per se but defines *plan* as "a method for accomplishing an objective." The term *strategy* has multiple definitions. The primary definition has a definite military application: "the science and art of military command aimed at meeting the enemy under conditions advantageous to one's own forces." That's it!

> *GOD-CENTERED strategic planning is a disciplined, intentional effort to develop and follow a method to accomplish God's objective for His church in order to meet the enemy under conditions that give us the advantage.*

Paul reminds us in his letter to the church at Ephesus that "our battle is not against flesh and blood, but against the rulers, against the authorities, against the world powers of this darkness, against the spiritual forces of evil in the heavens" (Eph 6:12). The women's ministry of the church is not just another program. It is making disciples for the kingdom of God. It is carrying out God's plan, which has eternal ramifications. We are in a spiritual battle, and the enemy will do what he can to move the church off course. Many times one of the enemy's most effective tactics is to draw the church into a laissez-faire attitude, convincing us that everything is fine.

Solomon warned that we are continually to be on the lookout for the little foxes that enter our vineyard. If we do not stay alert, before we know it, our vineyard will be invaded, trampled down, and destroyed by little foxes.

THREE EASY STEPS

Strategic planning is ongoing and continual. It is not something to be done in one day or a on a leadership retreat and then checked off a to-do list. Planning is a process. Strategic planning may be

---

[3] K. Hemphill and B. Taylor, *Ten Best Practices to Make Your Sunday School Work* (Nashville: Lifeway Church Resources), 25.

accomplished in three easy steps. Well, OK, maybe not so easy. However, there are three essential steps within the process of strategic planning: (1) determining what God wants us to be and do, and where to go, (2) mapping out the course, and (3) setting sail.

DETERMINING WHO, WHAT, AND WHERE

In his book *AquaChurch,* Leonard Sweet states, "Every successful [ministry] is successful in its own way. However we may try to pass ministries off as our own intuitive insights, settling for mimicry and impersonation only offers up a recipe for extinction."[4] Too many women's ministries today jump on the latest program, Bible study, or methodology bandwagon without realizing where that parade is taking them. The ultimate goal for which God wants a local church to aim will dictate how the women's ministry of the church is carried out. The church's responsibility is to execute the ministry in the best possible way to reach that goal, regardless of what everyone else may be doing.

A local church that is a New Testament church has been placed by God at a particular time, in a particular place, with an ability to reach a particular people. A church in San Jose, California, is able to reach a particular people to which a church in Tyler, Texas, may not have access. Florida works in a culture that is different from the culture of a church in Minnesota. A church in Minnesota has opportunities to reach people in 2009 that the same church did not have in 1959. Each local body of believers is unique, and God has a unique way of carrying out His ultimate plan in that context. Likewise, the women's ministry within that local church has a unique way of carrying out its purpose within the church.

Identify the church's mission and vision. The place to start in determining the who, what, and where is to identify the mission and vision of the church. Many churches will have both mission and vision statements where the mission statement is a short, easy to remember statement that communicates to both those outside the

---

[4] L. Sweet, *AquaChurch* (Loveland, CO: Group, 1999), 257.

church and those inside the church. The vision statement may be longer, expands the mission statement, and communicates more directly to the membership (see diagram 1).

If your church does not have a formal mission or vision statement, visit with your pastor or senior minister and ask him to share with you the mission God has given him for the church. Once you have a good grasp of the mission and vision of the church, then begin to pray about and determine the purpose of the women's ministry. What is God calling the women's ministry to be and do in order to help your church accomplish the vision of the church? This becomes the filter through which every event, program, and ministry is funneled. Too many ministries are doing a lot but very little truly related to accomplishing its purpose and mission.

Recognize spiritual markers. Many times in the Old Testament, God instructed His children to place stones or markers at places where He did an amazing work. The purpose of these markers was to remind the generations that followed of all that God had done. There is a time to look back and to see the markers that signify moments in time that have brought the ministry to where it is today. One spiritual marker might be the first women's Bible study offered or the first mission project the women did together. One of the markers might be the first leadership team formed. Every ministry develops through different journeys. It is important to acknowledge those markers and celebrate the work God has done. This will help to give you a sense of the path God currently has you on.

Conduct a SWOT analysis. SWOT stands for strengths, weaknesses, opportunities, and threats. This is a time for an honest, constructive evaluation of the ministry and the community the ministry serves. Strengths and weaknesses are generally areas to which change can be effected and are somewhat controllable. Ask, "What does this women's ministry do well, or what are we known for?" Conversely, ask, "Where are our weaknesses or gaps?" These questions are best answered by gaining feedback from those in the ministry. It often takes a leader being open to loving criticism and evaluation to allow a spotlight to be shown on blind spots.

Opportunities and threats are generally more external and reflect the church or community as a whole. An opportunity may be a change in the community that can provide a new area of ministry. For example, a church is located near a community college that is predominantly commuter students. Through the years the college has grown and is now building numerous student apartments and is transitioning to a more residential university. This becomes an opportunity to minister to college women. Being aware of these opportunities places the women's ministry in the position to act quickly. Many times the doors to these new opportunities are open for a short time, and only those leaders who see them opening are able to take advantage.

Threats are those things that can have a negative impact on a ministry. An example of this occurred in a church that was located near a military base. Military families made up almost 60 percent of its membership. When the government began to close military bases throughout the United States, they soon learned that the base near the church was one to be closed. The church, and the women's ministry, realized they would soon be losing a significant portion of their membership due to military transfers. A threat does not necessarily mean doom and gloom unless you get caught unaware. Rather, when you know it is coming, the leader can begin preparing for it and even turn threats into opportunities of ministry. A SWOT analysis is one of the most important evaluations a ministry can take. It is during this analysis that God often reveals new directions and areas that can be strengthened and helps propel ministries to the next level.

Identifying the target. When you have clarified the women's ministry's purpose and how it relates to the mission of the church, identified the spiritual markers, and conducted a SWOT analysis, a picture should be coming into focus. As you have sought the Lord's guidance through each of these steps, you will begin to see the path God is opening up before you. Are there new ministries to start? Weaknesses to correct? Strengths to continue to build upon? This is when the plan for the next year or two begins to unfold. Begin identifying two or three areas to focus on this year. For example, one church discovered it had a number of women who were attending church by themselves and were not a part of a Sunday school or small-group Bible study. Another church identified the need to train more leaders to be ready for an opportunity that was coming. And still another clearly knew this was the year to focus on evangelism. This is not the time to do everything at one time or even in one year. Ask the Lord to show you exactly what needs to be accomplished this year.

Mapping Out the Course

Now that you have identified the areas to focus on this year, it is time to map out the course. It is one thing to know what your destination will be. It is another thing to know how to get there. Bobb Biehl writes, "Leadership is knowing what to do next, knowing why that's important and knowing how to bring the appropriate resources on the need at hand."[5]

Set objectives and goals. For each area that you want to focus upon this year, set specific objectives and goals. An objective is what you want to accomplish, and goals are the specific steps needed to reach the objective. Objectives and goals should be as specific as possible with expected completion dates for each. As an example, let's take an area mentioned earlier. You have discovered that there are a number of women attending the Sunday morning worship service without their husbands, but they are not involved in a Sunday school class or small-group Bible study. The reasons their husbands don't attend vary. Some husbands work on Sundays; others are not believers or have just quit going to church. Still others are separated or in the midst of a divorce.

---

[5] Bobb Biehl, *Masterplanning* (Nashville: Broadman & Holman, 1997), 61.

OBJECTIVE: To have one Sunday morning women's Bible study by the first Sunday in January.

Note the specific action with a specific date. Once the objective is set, then work on the goals or steps needed to make this happen.

GOALS:

1. *Enlist the director and teacher by September 1.*
2. *Identify meeting location by September 15.*
3. *Select and order curriculum by October 1.*
4. *Identify potential class members by November 1.*
5. *Begin announcements December 1.*
6. *Begin making personal phone calls and invitations December 1.*

Like the objectives each goal is specific and dated. Dating each objective and goal provides a built-in checkpoint to ensure that you are moving in the right direction. Just remember, every goal helps accomplish an objective. Each objective helps accomplish the purpose of the women's ministry, which helps the church accomplish its mission and vision.

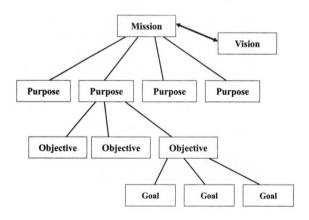

Diagram 1: Relationship of Mission, Purpose, Objectives, and Goals

Determine programming, scheduling, resources, and organization. Leaders are by nature visionaries. Not every vision will fit into the overall scheme of the church. For each area that you are focusing on and each objective that is set, make sure that it fits within the programming, scheduling, and organization of the church. The summer months, for many churches, are a time for focusing upon children and youth ministries. All of the camps, mission trips, Vacation Bible Schools, and special events can consume a great deal of the church's resources. That is probably not the best time to launch a huge women's ministry program that also requires resources. Scheduling is especially important for women's ministries. Because of the demands from home, the holiday times or end of school may not be a good time for women. Make sure the plans and goals that have been set fit within the program, schedule, and organization of the church.

Get creative and don't be afraid to risk. You have been created in the image of a creative God. You are a creative being. Do not let yourself get stuck in the box. Think outside the box. In fact, throw that box away! Some of the best solutions to accomplishing a goal are discovered through brainstorming sessions where anything is allowed to be put on the table. Many times the craziest ideas are just the sparks needed to come up with the answer. Do not get caught in the trap of always saying no or immediately dismissing an idea. Remember, the message of the gospel never changes, but there are an infinite number of ways to share that message with a lost world.

SETTING SAIL

You know where you are going, and you have mapped out the course. It is time to lift anchor and set sail. A lot of great plans are still sitting in the conference room because no one ever picked them up, entered the coordinates, and pushed off from the shore. There is a time for planning, and there is a time for implementation. If you have mapped it out correctly, it should be clear what the first step is to be. Once you have taken that first step, then take the next. Along the way keep checking the map to track your progress, evaluate how it is going, and continually check with the Lord.

Track your progress. The dates on the objective and goals that you have set now serve as checkpoints along the way. If you are starting that Sunday morning women's Bible study and it is now September 25 but you do not have a teacher yet, then you know you are a little behind. Track the numbers. Numbers are not everything, but they do tell us something. It will help you determine if you are reaching the women you intend to reach. Tracking is an ongoing process. Similar to taking a long trip to a place you have never been, you must check the map periodically to make sure you are still headed in the right direction.

Evaluate and refine along the way. Tracking helps you stay on the right road. Evaluation helps you know if the road you are on is getting you to the right place. The data collected and checkpoints that you track will help you evaluate whether the plans you have implemented are really accomplishing the goal. At least once a year, every element of the women's ministry should be evaluated by the leadership team. A good evaluation tool to use is shown in diagram 2.

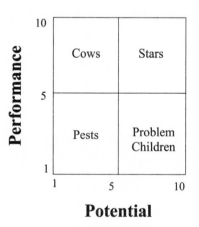

Diagram 2: Evaluation Matrix

Plot every event, Bible study, publication, and ministry that is considered part of the women's ministry on this diagram. For each evaluated item, the leadership team must come to an agreement on how the element being evaluated performed as opposed to its potential. Once everything is plotted, determine into which quadrant each falls. Then, the rule of thumb is to polish the stars, feed the cows, solve the problems, and get rid of the pests. "Stars" are those things that are going well, but just a little more polishing can make them even better. There is always room for improvement. "Cows" were not expected to go well, but they surprised everyone and exceeded expectations. To "feed the cows," send more resources to those areas in order to move them to a higher level of expected performance. The "problem children" are those things that were expected to perform well but fell below expectations. This indicates that there was a problem. Discover what the problem was (scheduling, weather, keynote speaker, etc.), solve that problem, and then try it again. "Pests" were not expected to do well, and they met expectations by not doing well. It is time either to get rid of a pest or significantly change it to increase expectation and performance. A recent example of a "pest" that a women's ministry faced was its monthly newsletter. The women's ministry always did a monthly newsletter even though everyone knew that few really read it. When the newsletter was evaluated, it clearly fell in the "pest" quadrant. The decision had to be made either to scrap the newsletter altogether or significantly change it. The final decision was to stop mailing out paper newsletters and to move it to being posted on the Web site and e-mailed to their members. Readership increased as they were able to add more color, graphics, and links. Pests can be changed into rising stars.

Be aware of "sacred cows." There are times when you know course corrections are necessary, or you discover a "pest" that needs to be dealt with. But in the process of making adjustments, you meet resistance because this is important to a significant group in your church. You may have stumbled upon a "sacred cow"—a ministry or program that is so meaningful to a group of people that if you were to change or discontinue this ministry, it would have far-reaching ramifications for you and the church. Jesus gave a warning for such times: "First sit down and calculate the cost" (Luke 14:28).

The Ruth class was mine. This group of older ladies had been together as a small group for decades. They met in a sizable room on the bottom floor next to the preschool area. The Ruth class had painted, hung curtains, and furnished the room with tables, lamps, and comfy chairs. They just loved their meeting room. As our church was growing, I had my eye on that space for a preschool room to expand child care for our women's Bible study. I located a new space for the Ruth class that I felt would be more than adequate. But when I approached these sweet ladies about the move, I quickly understood what this might cost me. The Ruth class was one of my biggest supporters and prayer warriors. I knew if this were not handled correctly it could have significant consequences. I did eventually move them, but it was on a much slower timetable. I spent almost a full year visiting and working with the ladies (especially the matriarch of the group), bringing them handmade Christmas cards from the preschoolers, sharing our vision for the women's ministry, especially the ministry to preschool moms, and involving the ladies in finding a space with which they were comfortable. I was even able to move all of their furniture and use the same curtains. It took a lot of work and time, but in the end it was worth it.

It is possible to change and even discontinue groups or ministries that need to be changed even when they have deep stakeholder roots. When faced with this task, ask yourself, "Is the cost of leaving a 'sacred cow' in place less than what it would cost us if we changed it?" A cost can be felt in loss of membership, loss of trust, loss of credibility, and even loss in finances. Sometimes the women's ministry (and you) are better off letting a "sacred crow" continue to graze until it dies a natural death.

There are many ways to evaluate a ministry. However you do it, the important thing is to do it. Evaluation allows course corrections to be made and places the ministry in a proactive stance rather than a reactive stance, thereby reducing the number of unplanned detours.

Continually check with the Lord. Leonard Sweet details in his book *AquaChurch* how early sailing captains would frequently check their position by locating the North Star. That was their constant, guiding light, and they checked it often. Our guiding light is Jesus Christ. He is the head and authority of all we do. He is the one who has given us the destination and helped us map out the course. Every day, without fail, we must check our position in relationship to where Christ is, making sure that our sails are turned in the right direction.

It is true that failing to plan is planning to fail. We live in a day when the assault against the Church and against the family is real. If we do not have a plan in place to reach women for Christ, help them grow in their faith, and become involved in ministry, then we are nothing more than a women's club who enjoys their tea parties and get-togethers. We do not have a choice to plan or not to plan. Planning forces us to ask the question, "Is this ministry going to affect the future at random and stay the same old thing or will we step out with purpose and allow God to take us to the next level?"

QUESTIONS FOR DISCUSSION

1. Based upon a study of Scripture, how do strategic planning and dependence upon the leading of the Holy Spirit go hand in hand?
2. What are the struggles that leaders face to plan adequately today?
3. What are the strengths, weaknesses, opportunities, and threats that face your women's ministry today?
4. There are other ways to evaluate ministries than the evaluation matrix presented here. What other tools can be used to evaluate effectively a ministry and its programs?

Chapter 13

Enlisting the Team

Jaye Martin

For as the body is one and has many parts, and
all the parts of that body, though many, are one
body—so also is Christ (1 Cor 12:12).

I never understood the importance of a team until years after I
served with my church as the women's ministry leader. The
team that I began with was one of godly women who had a
passion for God and a passion for women. Some were Bible study
teachers, some visionaries, some with a passion for missions and
prayer, some with an incredible gift of service, and all committed to
making a difference in the kingdom. I cannot take credit for building
this team because it was there when I started. My pastor's wife and
another godly woman had seen the need for women's ministry. They
prayed and God brought the team together.

It was years later before I realized how hard it is to build a team
and lead them to serve together. The principles in this chapter are
ones that I learned from serving there and from now working with
teams across our great nation. No matter where you begin, with an
existing team or by building them one by one, it all must begin with

prayer. God is the one who puts teams together. He is the one who knows what your church needs and who needs to serve with you. I don't say this lightly because God is the foundation for ministry and especially for enlisting and building teams.

Enlisting a team is something that looks easy but can be quite challenging to do. Most of us inherit teams and don't have the luxury of building our own. Somehow in the early years of ministry, I thought a team was just having a list of jobs to do and enlisting women to be in charge of each area of ministry. If I had my list and a leader for each area, I thought I was finished. It is quite humorous looking back on it all now. In this chapter we will begin with the team leader, deal with the purpose of the team, look at how to choose your team, see how to provide the best environment for the team to operate in, and look at some of the ways to build unity on your team. Enlisting a team is a lot more than filling slots, and this chapter will give you just a glance at how to enlist team members for your leadership team.

While *team* is not a word used in the Bible, the concept of working together in groups toward a purpose or goal is certainly found throughout Scripture. One of my favorite passages is found in Mark 3 when Jesus called together His team of disciples. "Then He went up the mountain and summoned those He wanted, and they came to Him. He also appointed 12—He also named them apostles—to be with Him, to send them out to preach, and to have authority to drive out demons" (Mark 3:13–15). He clearly called out some from the crowd and they came. He then appointed the Twelve so that they could "be with Him." He also gave them a purpose—to preach—and gave them the authority to do so, in His power of course. Even in these few verses we see the basic concepts of appointing the team, spending time with the team transferring truths, communicating the purpose of the team, and empowering the team to act.

As we look at the concept of building and leading a team, it all begins with the leader. In our fourth and fifth chapters, we looked at the general characteristics of leadership as well as the uniqueness of women in leadership. The foundation of a team is based on the leader herself. We see this concept clearly in sports. Coaches are given credit for the success or failure of the team to win. When the team has too many losses, the coach is likely to be let go. Leadership is the key to winning teams. As we look at building a team of women to work within the local church, we must begin with some essential qualities of the team leader.

CHARACTERISTICS OF THE TEAM LEADER

A leader must first know who she is. She needs to know her spiritual giftedness, understand her personality, be aware of her strengths and weaknesses, and understand the season of life in which she finds herself. These things are foundational. The leader also needs to be secure in who she is in Christ, be Spirit-filled on a daily basis, and be a good listener. She must understand not only the task or purpose of the team but understand the importance of believing in team members to accomplish those goals. She has to see tasks and people. Clarity is important in both. All the tasks of ministry are important, but equally important are those on the team with whom the leader works and those that the team serves in ministry.

Having worked for many years, including more than 20 in ministry, I have served on numerous teams. Most often I was a part of a team or staff as a member while also leading my own team of women. I have learned the hard way about what makes for a strong, functioning, and balanced team as well as what makes for a dysfunctional one. The best leaders are those who know how to follow and be a part of the team in addition to knowing what makes a good leader.

TEAM PURPOSE

Every team needs to be clear about its purpose. It is up to the team leader to communicate to the team what the purpose is and why the team exists. When I was asked to lead the women's ministry at my church, the administration was clear in several things about what our purpose would be. Yes, they wanted us to be involved in ministry to women, but the purpose that was communicated over and over again to me was that the women were out from under authority. I was being hired, in part, to bring them in and to oversee them and make sure that they were following church policies and procedures. I felt like the youth minister getting in trouble for the youth who were running down the halls during the service. How could I possibly communicate to the wonderful ladies that several of them were completely out of line when it came to church operations? Events had been planned but never approved by church staff. There had been plans for a women's breakfast, but the banquet room had not been reserved, and the food service people had not been notified. Event signs with lace would appear all over the church but with no understanding about what else was happening in the church. While the staff was 100 percent behind women's ministry, the ministry was in jeopardy because many of these women felt what they were planning was more important than anything going on. If "God told them to have the event," then they could not understand what the problem was. Other ministries were expected to have no needs and the staff needed someone to communicate all of this, so basically they hired me to do just that. Of course, no one told me until after I had signed on the dotted line.

In order to share this with my inherited team of women, I had to have God's help. I prayed and prayed, and at last it came to me. These women were godly, wonderful women. They did not intend to be out from under authority; they just had a passion to do what God had called them to do. We had monthly meetings for our team leaders, and every month I tried to share the plan of what was needed before we could do an event or even schedule a Bible study. It seems that every month I dealt with this to no avail. I was constantly finding myself sitting in the office of one of my supervisors while he told me who was going around the system. Finally it came to me. One meeting I told my leaders to wear hats to the meeting. Any type of hat would do. It became a topic of conversation of what kind of hat each would wear. The meeting day finally came, and these ladies showed up in every kind of hat you could imagine: an Easter bonnet, a prairie woman hat, a baseball cap, a cowboy hat, and a host of others. We shared about our hats, and finally it was my turn to share why we were wearing hats. We were under authority. That was it. We were to remember that the reason we could do what we did was that we had been granted permission by God but also by those He had placed in authority over us. I reminded them that it was, in fact, a privilege to be under authority. We had both protection and provision in that place. We were not forgotten. No one was out to get us. We were there to minister to women. We were there to model what it meant to be in submission. I was there to help communicate to the staff just what we needed and why, but I must be in submission to my leaders and that they must, in turn, let me be in the loop. They needed to report to me. I was not there to make things difficult; I was there to make our ministry more effective as well as more efficient. We were to get our leaders that we enlisted approved in advance so that if there were a problem with someone, our ministry would be protected. Wow. They got it. At least most of them did. Remembering the hat meeting became a fun memory. We were going to keep our hats on and remember that we were there for the purpose of ministry but also for the purpose of the church as a whole.

Even though I inherited a team in my church, the ministry did not have a clear purpose. The ministry had been formally started about nine months before I came. There was no question that it was founded on biblical principles, and lots of things were happening. Now it was time to formulate a clear sense of direction. I knew that we needed to have a mission statement and a focus. To be able to build and develop the team, the purpose would need to be clear. Having been to seminary and having thought some about the purpose of ministries, I knew exactly where we needed to go. However, I also knew that being the youngest one and spanking new, that I had to lead them to discover their purpose. We had a series of meetings that included praying for God to show us His purpose, looking at what the Scriptures had to say about church and the purpose for women ministering to women, brainstorming through various topics and ideas, and praying some more. When the time came that I knew they understood the need, I shared with them the purpose of reaching women, nurturing women, involving women, and supporting the church while we mentored others. God's purpose became our purpose. We were unified and clear on what we needed to do and could concentrate on when and where we needed to be. A verse was suggested by our pastor's wife and women's ministry advisor, and it became our mission statement: "For we are His creation— created in Christ Jesus for good works, which God prepared ahead of time so that we should walk in them" (Eph 2:10). This verse along with our list of tasks helped us to communicate our purpose and to give reason when someone wanted to do something that was not a part of what God had called us to do. It allowed us to say no when needed. Instead of doing good things, we could focus on doing the best things.

CHOOSING A TEAM

The selection of teammates should be an exciting time for all concerned. It should also be a strategic time. When you understand yourself as a leader, you are best able to understand a little more about what you need and whom you want to serve with you. As you begin to pray about whom you want to include, it is important to note some other characteristics for which to look. Before these women are enlisted, it will be important to get approval for them from your supervisor. Most churches will have an approval process, and you will want to be careful to follow it. The approval process is in place for the protection of the members. It allows the staff or committee to make sure that capable leaders are in the right place of service for them and for the ministry.

TEAM MEMBER CHARACTERISTICS

One of the first things to consider is who. Whom do you want on your team? What woman or women do you know that you would want to serve with you? After praying, this might be one of the first things that you do: talk to this person and see what her gifts are and what she might be interested in leading. Some might say that enlistment should begin with defining the job description and then looking for someone who fits. Let me suggest to you that you can do that, and certainly many staff search committees do just that, but that I would first look for the right godly woman or women who you know are trusted and loyal servants of Christ. See where they fit best for service and mold the jobs around these women. You will find that this will keep the team dynamic and flowing. Teams that just fill positions are more likely to have a hard time working together than those that are built and mobilized by giftedness. God is a creative and dynamic God, and He has a way of meeting the needs of every ministry by putting the right leaders in place at the right time.

I have a lady who has served with me for years in my evangelism ministry. She and I are perfect complements to each other. My heritage is Christianity for generations back. Her heritage is that none were believers, and she came to Christ at the age of 22, never before having heard the name of Jesus. She was already married with several children. God wove our lives together in many ways, and so when we equip women to share Christ, women can hear the challenges from a Christian and from a lost perspective. She is also a lover of people, and they love her. After we teach, she usually has a long line of women waiting to talk to her. She is outgoing and relational and a good complement to me. Over the years we have looked for others to add to our team of national trainers. When we add someone, we make sure they have what the two of us don't. In my national ministry I also look for a diversity of ages, women from different regions of the country, ethnicity, educational levels, as well as spiritual giftedness. I look for women with a passion for the ministry. I can teach skills, but I cannot teach passion. That is something that God has to do. Just because a lady has a skill set does not mean that she is a good fit for the team. Look for women who are gifted and for women who have a passion to serve with you and serve with you for the glory of God rather than for their own glory or any other motive.

After you select the first few members of your team, you will then be able to divide the tasks of the ministry and know better whom you want to join you and what you want them to do. As you pray together, it will be exciting to see whom God brings to join you. When I did evangelism ministry in the local church, I remember vividly praying for God to see people join the church who were trained leaders in evangelism. It was awesome to see God actually bring people to join our church who were already trained communicating to us that God had led them there. Even though this was an unadvertised need, we had members calling to volunteer to be trained in evangelism. When you pray for leaders, God really does raise them up. He builds the team. The leader must continue to be open to the working of the Holy Spirit in the crucial development of the team. The team leader must also be willing to wait on the timing to add new leaders. Ministries should not be started until there is a leader with a passion for that ministry area.

One of the things I really felt the Lord wanted in my women's ministry in the local church was to have a leader who would take all the craft, quilting, and cooking classes and make them evangelistic. Our church had numbers of classes designed to reach out, but all were not led by evangelistic leaders. I thought we needed a woman who would lead in this area, especially since we had a lot of seniors who would love to be involved. It was years before God brought that person to lead that ministry, but it was well worth the wait.

I mention age because in order to reach women of different ages, you must have a variety of ages involved. If you want young women involved, you have to have several involved in key leadership areas. I have found that it works well to have older and younger women teamed to lead in every ministry area. This way they can teach each other. The older can be a Titus 2 mentor while the younger can help the older to gain valuable insights in how to reach her generation.

In the diverse world in which we live, it is important to have an ethnically diverse leadership team. Living in Houston, I am used to diversity in my church, neighborhood, and basically everywhere I go. As I travel in the United States and Canada, I am amazed at the lack of diversity in so many areas. Our churches need to reflect the diversity in the community. Leaders must make a concerted effort to reach out and look for leaders to be involved. Regardless of what ethnicity you or your church are, you should intentionally cross cultures and reach out to those who are not like you. There is nothing wrong with being in groups like ourselves except when these groups keep us from being inclusive or keep ourselves from reaching people for Christ. I feel sure that when we get to heaven, it will include all nations and people groups. The Internet has brought more global awareness, and our new postmodern world is demanding diversity. If our churches are going to reach the postmodern generation, we had better get with the program. I know that God is pleased when we make a commitment to reach all nations and begin by looking for leaders that He brings.

The same problem can exist not only in diversity of race but also in economic status. As we look at our team leaders, it will be important to make sure that we are inclusive of all types of women. Spirit-filled leaders don't have to have a certain amount of money. Those of lesser means are a good reminder of the blessings we have plus the need to be sensitive when planning events to provide lower costs and scholarships as needed.

Even in the local church, it is important that educational level be included as you look at characteristics for women leaders. It is great to have some women who are highly educated, but it is just as great to have some who never had the opportunity to finish high school. Women come from all walks of life, and sometimes we exclude women without even meaning to do so. I have seen so many godly women come to the seminary campus to visit who are intimidated because of their lack of a master's degree. I feel strongly that a master's can be important but am sure that when we get to heaven, it will not be one of the criteria for entrance or placement on the heavenly team.

Season of life is something about which we don't hear enough. It is important to ask women to lead and take on responsibility that is conducive to their season of life. One should not ask a young wife and mother of three to take on the day-to-day workings of a huge event. This is not to say that she is not capable of doing this but to say that we should not put her in the position to lead a major event while she is overcommitted at home. There may be cases where the situation would allow this, but it is usually better if the one who takes on these major events is in a season of life that permits her time to commit to the task at hand. As an empty nester for the past few years, I have found that I can take on much more than I could when my daughter was in high school. In fact, as a grade-school mom, I probably had much more time than when my daughter was a preschooler and even more time than when she was in middle school. I am fortunate that my parents and my husband's parents are in good health, but many of my friends find themselves in the sandwich generation, squeezed between kids and aging parents. These women in this season need to be able to be involved but must lessen the load carried by leadership roles at church. A single mom has major priorities of children and usually works. She needs to be involved in leadership in creative ways that work for her and her family. I have found that since I work, things at church that involve e-mail communication are ideal for me. I can do this late into the evening and when I travel. While it is difficult to involve women in different seasons, it is important not to write women off if they cannot make the Tuesday morning meeting. I continue to hear of teams meeting in creative ways and at creative times. There are ways to involve everyone, regardless of her season of life.

Almost a given in picking members of a team is the area of spiritual giftedness. There are numerous spiritual gift inventories. Make sure the inventory that you use is from a reliable source and have copies available for the new members of your church. When women join the church, it is a great time to involve them in some aspect of ministry based on their spiritual gifts. A team that has every gift represented in one or more of the leaders will be a well-functioning team. If you happen to be an administrator, you will want to have one or several with the gift of service. At the seminary I am on a team with a great variety of gifts represented in about five people.

We are lacking in one gift. I just made the comment that the next person we add should be someone with this giftedness because it is obvious to me that we are lacking in this area. When building a team, it is usually easy to find those with the gift of leadership, teaching, shepherding, and encouragement to add to the team. It can be difficult to know how to utilize some of the other gifts. Look for those with a variety of gifts, and see how you can help them plug into the team that you build.

Another thing to look for when building a team is ministry involvement. Look for someone who is already involved in ministry. You might, at times, find someone who needs to be involved. Often your best leaders are right under your nose. They are already involved in the classes, events, prayer groups, and other things that you offer. Be careful about taking someone from no ministry involvement to leading in the ministry. Rarely does this work, especially with women. You certainly can bring someone in who has not been involved before, but in most cases women's leaders come from within the organization or ministry. The faithful woman who has been coming to every Bible study offered for years is probably more than ready to take on something. It might be that she begins to organize the room, greets attendees, becomes the assistant teacher, or assumes another job. Ministries are full of people just waiting to be asked to serve.

The need for spiritual maturity is of the utmost priority in every situation. Scripture is clear about not putting someone in a leadership position who does not have the spiritual maturity to be able to handle it. We may want to include younger leaders, but they should not be included in ways that will set them up for failure. Use them in tasks that involve leadership, use them for specific assignments, use them in creative ways, but do not put them in overseeing positions before they are ready.

We looked at the season of life as an important factor, but another similar issue is simply the time factor. A working woman who is married just does not have as much time as a widow who doesn't hold a job outside the home. A woman who is already the chairman of a bunch of committees and committed to several ministries does not have as much time as one who is only involved in the ministry to women. As you enlist leaders, be sure to communicate how much time the job and involvement in the ministry will take. I will never forget signing up for something when my daughter was in kindergarten. I thought I was offering to help with something in her classroom. It turned out that I was offering to colead one of the major fund-raising events of the school. It was so embarrassing trying to explain my way out of it over and over again when I would have been so much better off just asking a few questions before I put my name on that piece of paper that was passed around.

Who is willing to serve? Who is available to serve? These sound like no-brainer questions, but they are important ones to ask. Some women will just not be willing or able to serve in leadership. Willingness and availability to serve are essential. With my travel schedule I am limited in where and when I can serve at my church. Leadership has always been great to work with me given my time constraints. I am willing to serve but just not available. I know some women who are available but really don't want to serve.

It is important to offer different levels and layers of leadership. As you look for team leaders, it is important to offer different levels of commitment. Maybe you have some jobs that are larger and some smaller, some that require weekend time and some during weekdays or weeknights. By offering lots of different levels of involvement, more will be able to participate.

JOB DESCRIPTIONS

Job descriptions are important for any team. You may enlist several women for your team, but sometime as the team is forming, job descriptions should be established. These descriptions may be fluid, but they should be put in place. Change is a part of every situation that is growing so it is important that every leader understand that jobs may change according to the needs of the church. Communication will become even more important as tasks are shared, new opportunities arise, and new leaders come on board. The young lady who serves as my assistant at the seminary has a completely different set of gifts from the lady who worked with me previously. This is usually the case since each person brings a different set of gifts and experiences. When my new assistant started, we took personality inventories and talked about our giftedness. We determined who would do what based on that. There are times when I have to deal with something because I am the director and times when it falls in her court because she is the assistant, but for the most part we try to do the things in which we are stronger. As you have new women added to the team, it may be necessary to look again at who is good at what and adjust your job descriptions accordingly.

FINDING LEADERS

One of the questions I hear from coast to coast is, "How do I find leaders?" Looking for volunteer leaders is common to just about every ministry area. To find leaders and effective team members, let me suggest a few don'ts and then a few do's. Don't make an announcement asking for volunteers. The women who respond may not be the ones that would be best in your ministry. Don't find your best friends and guilt them into serving because you think it would be more fun. Don't enlist your extended family members to serve because you are desperate for help. To find God's leaders for your team, begin with some serious prayer time. Pray alone and pray with other ministry leaders. Seek God's input and know that He will bring the right leaders to serve with you. Take the time to ask your pastor and others one-on-one if they know of godly women who might be gifted in particular areas of service. Look for who is already involved in your ministry or others who might have the potential for leadership. Look for women who are faithful with what they have been given and are ready for the next step of service. Look for the right motive of those who are serving. Motive is of the utmost importance. Look for women who understand what it means to follow God and glorify Him—selfless servant leaders who want what God wants. Look for those who might need to be involved. Look for older and younger women who can serve and lead together.

Leadership Covenants

One helpful thing in enlisting leaders is having a covenant or agreement that leaders sign before serving. This covenant can include many things such as length of service, job descriptions, spiritual preparedness, meetings or duties agreed to, and the like. Some believe that every team leader and ministry leader should sign one. Others would say that covenants are nonessentials. I believe that it depends on the situation and the job and task at hand. Covenants have their place. They bring with them a sense of professionalism, expected behavior, and commitment. For teachers of Bible study classes, it can be most helpful to know the length of service and exactly what is expected. For another job, such as a one-time event coordinator, it might not be as necessary. Either way, the important part is to communicate what is expected to each leader.

As leaders and team members are enlisted, I suggest that a trial period be established even before covenants are signed. Trial periods allow the person to see if she fits the position of leadership and also allow the removal of the leader before it becomes too late and so harder to move the person. Sometimes women are not good fits for the position for which they have been enlisted. If a woman is being enlisted to lead the prayer ministry, it might be helpful to ask her to lead it for a semester and see if it is a fit for her. This allows open communication during the trial period, and problems can be addressed. There is no shame in leading something for a semester. If the woman works well in the position, she can be enlisted to lead for another year or so. If the woman would be a better fit somewhere else, she can be given another position as the need arises. I have created many new jobs for women over the years. It is amazing how God opens the doors and does the best for everyone involved when we seek His leadership in delicate situations.

Leading Leaders and Team Building

Supervising leaders on your ministry team can be much like raising a child. When a baby is born, the baby needs the mother's milk or formula. New mothers tend to stay close to new babies. As the baby grows, the child starts to eat some cereal and then soft baby foods. When the body is ready, the baby eats some mushy food and grows into eating adult food. This happens over a period of time. The mother is able to be away a little longer until the child is weaned. The same process applies to new ministries and especially new leaders. As a new leader begins, she may need a lot of help and supervision. The first few weeks of teaching are major preparation times that usually come with lots of questions. The new teacher may make many mistakes, but she is learning. As the leader learns, you as a ministry director will be able to move away, and she will be less dependent on you. The younger the leader (in terms of experience), the more time will be needed overseeing her. The more experience she has should allow you to move away and not be as actively involved. When a leader is seasoned, she will still need you just as an adult woman still needs and longs for interaction with her mother.

CREATING A TEAM ENVIRONMENT

Team building is something that doesn't just happen. It involves much prayer, time, and commitment; and it means that an environment for team building must be created. Think about the teams of which you want to be a part. Chances are that these teams are exciting. They usually have a clear sense of purpose, and there are benefits to being a part of them. I have always loved the local church. Yes it has flaws, but everyone does. My local church is a team I love. The pastor is a born leader and a gifted teacher. He has a clear sense of calling and leads our church in being unapologetically evangelistic. His team of staff carries out his leadership in numerous areas of ministry, and his members serve by carrying out the ministry of the church. Our church is exciting because our pastor is excited on a daily basis about what God is doing in our midst. He has created an environment for everyone to be a part of the team. No matter who you are, you have ample opportunities for service. Some jobs are held for those especially gifted in teaching, but the masses can be involved in serving at some level. All of this comes about because of a commitment to prayer and to creating an environment for ministry and for the team.

Creating an environment involves leadership, direction, and excitement, but it also involves some other essentials. Leaders must be caring women who will listen and respect those who serve with them. Leaders must be continual learners and never stop changing to meet the growing needs of the women and the community. Confidentiality is also an important part of creating an environment for leadership. The team must learn to keep some things within the team and to give support to one another as needed. Balance in personal life as well as team life is important. Knowing when and how to balance all the needs of women takes much prayer and much time. Another aspect of the environment is the delegation factor. Leaders generally want to lead so you as the ministry director must be willing to delegate in order to get the best leaders possible. Strong leaders should not threaten us. Strong leaders build strong teams. I learned many years ago that in building a team, one must look for those who are outstanding in at least one area. Average women make average teams, but outstanding leaders make for outstanding teams. Teams are only as great as the women on them. Godly leaders who are tapped into God's plan, gifted for service in at least one area of leadership, and willing to serve are those with whom we need to serve. Part of creating the environment is creating the right team.

GROUP DYNAMICS AND TEAM-BUILDING ACTIVITIES

You will find many resources for team-building activities. Teams that play together seem to work well together. Look for things that your team can do together to get to know one another on a personal level. It is incredible to do ministry together, and true fellowship flows out of doing evangelism, discipleship, and ministry. Instead of each of your leaders just leading their ministry area, look for ways your team might serve together. It is important for the team to get to know one another by serving together.

There are many creative things a team can do to play together. Things like using a large kitchen and everyone working together to prepare a meal, working in a garden or painting a house, doing a fashion show from a resale shop or a community center, and numerous more known things like playing sports, doing ropes courses, or putting on a skit—all create fun while allowing the leaders to get to know one another.

No matter how well the group knows one another, there will always be issues. Because we are all sinful in nature, at times we will clash. This should be seen as a natural part of the group dynamics. The conflict will work itself out, especially when godly women handle conflict according to biblical principles, as we will discuss in the next chapter.

In Conclusion

Enlisting your team is a task that is never completed. It is a continual process. When I began serving as the leader of women's ministry at my church, I somehow thought that if I had a list of titles and jobs and if I filled all the slots, then my team-enlisting days would be over. After eight years on staff, I don't believe there was ever even one day when there was not a position open and in need of a leader. It seemed that it was a continual process that never ended. So look on team building as a continual, dynamic, and exciting process that allows you to see what God is doing and how He is using you to mobilize women for ministry. And thank God right now that it never ends. Enjoy every minute of your time with your leaders and pour yourself into them. When God calls one to move, you will know that you have just sent out the first missionary into the kingdom. They will go and lead and you will know that it is time to pour into others. Allow them to bless you in return.

Questions for Discussion

1. Read the passages on spiritual gifts in 1 Corinthians 12; Romans 12; and Ephesians 4. How do women with differing gifts, serving on the same team, work well together?

2. What are the spiritual and other characteristics that you need to look for when enlisting women to lead in the church?
3. What are some of the ways you might know a potential women's leader when you see one?
4. What are some creative ways you could lead your team to discover the purpose for the ministry to women?
5. How can you create a reaching, nurturing, ministering environment for team leadership among women?

Chapter 14

Living Through Change and Conflict

Jaye Martin

Look, I am about to do something new; even now it is
coming. Do you not see it? Indeed, I will make a way
in the wilderness, rivers in the desert (Isa 43:19).

A few people thrive on change. I admit to being one of them. You have to know that as you read through this chapter. Some people thrive on change, and for others change is their worst fear. Change is hard for most people. Unfortunately, change is often necessary in ministry. When change becomes essential, it can cause conflict. Conflict can be the result of change, but conflict can also be the result of two people just not seeing eye to eye. Some handle conflict better than others. I would not say that I like conflict, but it doesn't scare me. I do try to avoid it, but unfortunately, if there are two people, conflict is inevitable. In this chapter we will look at how to make the best of both change and conflict. Let's begin by looking first at change. Then we will talk about conflict.

IN THE BEGINNING, CHANGE . . .

From the beginning of the Bible in Genesis to the conclusion in Revelation, God painted a portrait of change. Creator God, all powerful, wrote just how it all began in Genesis 1:1–5.

> *In the beginning God created the heavens and the earth. Now the earth was formless and empty, darkness covered the surface of the watery depths, and the Spirit of God was hovering over the surface of the waters. Then God said, "Let there be light," and there was light. God saw that the light was good, and God separated the light from the darkness. God called the light "day," and He called the darkness "night." Evening came, and then morning: the first day (Gen 1:1–5).*

On that very first day, God changed things. God did not change, but everything else did. In Revelation 21:5a, He again reminded readers that in that final day, "Then the One seated on the throne said, 'Look! I am making everything new.'" The biblical text was clearly written; change was to be a part of life.

Why is it that we have difficulty dealing with something that has been around since the very beginning and will be around until the end of time? Change will never cease, so I will attempt to lay out some basic truths using the Bible as the foundation for how to handle change.

A BIBLICAL CASE STUDY ON CHANGE

While the Bible contains numerous passages about change, let's look at the story of Jesus' first miracle found in John 2:1–11. Jesus had been invited to a wedding feast and changed the water into wine. The symbolism appears so profound here. Read the following passage and look at how Jesus communicates and illustrates changing from the old to the new.

On the third day a wedding took place in Cana of Galilee.
Jesus' mother was there, and Jesus and His disciples
were invited to the wedding as well. When the wine
ran out, Jesus' mother told Him, "They don't have any
wine." "What has this concern of yours to do with Me,
woman?" Jesus asked. "My hour has not yet come." "Do
whatever He tells you," His mother told the servants.
Now six stone water jars had been set there for Jewish
purification. Each contained 20 or 30 gallons. "Fill the
jars with water," Jesus told them. So they filled them to
the brim. Then He said to them, "Now draw some out
and take it to the chief servant." And they did. When
the chief servant tasted the water (after it had become
wine), he did not know where it came from—though the
servants who had drawn the water knew. He called the
groom and told him, "Everybody sets out the fine wine
first, then, after people have drunk freely, the inferior. But
you have kept the fine wine until now." Jesus performed
this first sign in Cana of Galilee. He displayed His glory,
and His disciples believed in Him (John 2:1–11).

Jesus would change history by being raised from the dead on the third day, and John, the author, points to the resurrection and the ultimate change that was to come. Throughout the New Testament, the church is referred to as the bride of Christ. This symbolism arguably holds true in this passage as well. Jesus is there by invitation, and He must be invited for believers to have Him in their lives and experience the ultimate transformation of salvation. The old wine has gone. Not only do we see that in the physical sense—the group has run out of wine—but also in the spiritual sense, the old has gone. There is urgency to the situation. Since the hosts of the wedding party want to provide fulfillment for their guests, Jesus' mother wants Jesus to come to the rescue. She instructs the servants to follow Him and do what He says. It is a clear picture of being under Jesus' lordship. While Jesus shares that His time has not yet come, He asks the servants to bring the six jars (that were used for ceremonial cleansing) and says to fill them up with water. The imperfect number of six illustrates the old way of ceremonies and rituals. The water filling them becomes another point of illustration of how in the later days the Holy Spirit will fill the new believer and be the ultimate change agent. These jars, so full with water, have no room for anything else. The Holy Spirit will completely indwell the believer. At the word of Jesus, they drew the water for the master of the banquet. Not only had it turned to wine, but it also had turned into the very best wine. The grapes that had been crushed were now made into a fine wine that was more than ample for all. The reader might draw from this that people must be broken to be made new and that the best is yet to come. John showed us that Jesus revealed His glory on that third day and that His disciples put their faith in Him. It is quite a message of change communicated in a creative and tangible way.

SEEK GOD AND HIS TIMING

When the master of the wedding feast ran out of wine, it created an urgent situation. Jesus was able to use the incident to show a real need. While it was a physical need, the spiritual need was also there. Jesus most likely knew that the wine would run out, yet He let it. He did not rescue them before they were ready to see and hear what He had to say. As women leaders who see a need for change in a certain area, we must rely on God's provision for the change as well as His timing. Often we see the need for the change before the timing is actually right to follow through with it. God has a way of preparing His people, so allow Him to lead you as you look for how He will bring it to fruition.

SEEK WISE COUNSEL

At the wedding feast it is likely that numerous people from the community were there. Jesus changed enough water into wine that it would be enough to serve between two or three thousand cups. In addition to having a huge and captive audience, the disciples (His key players) were there and obviously got the message since they put their faith in Him. For us, when it comes to change, we must get input from God but also from wise counsel. Others who are more seasoned leaders should be consulted and heeded. God puts wise counsel there for us, and they have valuable insights that need to be considered.

SET THE DIRECTION

A vision tells where one is headed, and the strategy explains how one is going to get there. In developing a vision, it is necessary to be able to see from the present and into the future, if you will. For many the vision is difficult. It takes a gifted person to see what needs to happen and what it should look like. The strategy used to get there can be even more challenging. Some know where they need to go but have no idea what plans need to be put into place and how they should be implemented. Jesus already had a vision and a strategy that God had given Him. God sent Jesus to die for the sins of people by sacrificing His life on the cross. He also had to develop followers and send out the message of what God had in mind and the abundant life He could give. Jesus' mother was trying to rush the plan, but Jesus knew just the right timing needed. This would be the beginning of His ministry, not the end. Much more work still needed to be done in order to create action in the lives of others.

SHARE THE CHANGES

Jesus used the simplicity of the water and the wine to give a picture that would be remembered by all. In fact he used several object lessons that worked together to communicate His point. Not only did He use the water and the wine, but also the water pots themselves became object lessons. Such items illustrated the old and new covenants, the Holy Spirit's filling, the marriage and purity implied, and so forth. If the disciples did not pick up on all of these lessons, they would have had to see some of them. When the vision is shared during change, it needs to be shared in as many creative ways as possible. We surely did not see Jesus holding up a chart with a bunch of numbers. He communicated His truth in who He was and what He did. The whole wedding banquet became the illustration of the abundance that He would provide. The disciples were empowered to learn and eventually, when the time was right, to lead the way. They were the ones who would carry the message of Christ after His death, and Jesus needed them to begin to understand what was happening so that they would be ready to lead a few years later.

CHOOSE TO CHANGE

The wedding feast with the changing of the water into wine was just one of many memories that would carry the disciples through the difficult times. It would build momentum and give them something to focus on and remember when the going got tough.

Just because Jesus used the ceremonial cleansing water pots to make new wine did not mean that the spiritual event was over. The physical event was over, but in a spiritual sense things had just begun. The spiritual transformation process would make these disciples into the men that God wanted them to be. God would have to be allowed to do His work in each one. Each one would come to choose whether he would allow himself to be transformed.

CONTINUE TO CHANGE

Jesus did not stop His mission once change started. He kept going. The disciples had to choose to continue in the change they had started. The definition of change implies a constant motion.

Women must sell out and be transformed or changed themselves before they can help others to be change agents and lead real change in the church. Transformational leadership is the process of transformation in the life of the believer and leader and also leadership. With that, let me make the distinction that just because someone has been transformed does not mean that he or she is a great leader. While one can have a vibrant relationship with Christ, it does not mean that this same one has the necessary abilities to be a leader in a business sense. Leadership involves numerous things, and transformation is just the starting point for real leadership development.

CHANGE IS INEVITABLE

There will always be change. The real question may be, When is change necessary? or Do we really have to change? Certainly, every leader is asked this question. As a leader, you had better be sure you have a good answer before it comes up. I wish I could apply the "old and new wineskins" parable to change: "And no one puts new wine into old wineskins. Otherwise, the skins burst, the wine spills out, and the skins are ruined. But they put new wine into fresh wineskins, and both are preserved" (Matt 9:17). Often it seems that it would be so much easier just to start over.

Surely every ministry leader has thought about starting over at one time or another. I was asked to lead the women's ministry at my church. I had been there as a member since I graduated from college and moved to Houston some 11 years before so I had certainly been around awhile. Almost a year after I graduated from seminary, the church asked me to be the coordinator for the women. I had served in education, and my expertise was in evangelism, mostly working in the youth and college ministries. I had no idea what women's ministry was, but I did know that the women had just had a big tea party. I also knew that I did not want any part of it. It wasn't that I did not like tea parties, but to take my precious time as a wife, mom, and one who had been called from the insignificant to the significant to go to a meaningless tea just did not cut it for me. When I shared with my pastor's wife that I did not do tea parties, she informed me that there had already been a tea party and that we did not need another. Oh my, she was so patient with me. For every excuse I gave, she had an answer. After a week of telling her no, I finally told her that I might only stay a day and that I would change everything—and she agreed. Of course, she was desperate.

Upon agreeing to lead, we found ourselves facing numerous needed changes. First, there was no articulated purpose for the ministry. While each one involved had her own idea of what that purpose was, few were sharing the same vision. It caused me to go back to my Bible and search out the purpose of the church and especially of a ministry to women. I came to the strong conviction that writing a purpose statement would be the first step in knowing where the team needed to be led.

Instead of calling the team together and telling them exactly what we needed to change, I called the team to prayer. I asked other leaders to pray with us about what our purpose should be. We looked at the Scriptures and talked about the women in the Bible. It could have taken a long time, but in a few short months we came down to some basic truths. We came to the same conclusion—that God had a special plan for women. We chose Ephesians 2:10 as our verse: "For we are His creation—created in Christ Jesus for good works, which God prepared ahead of time so that we should walk in them." We decided that as a ministry we would reach women for Christ, mature them in the faith, involve them in ministry using spiritual gifts and talents, and support our church in the process. The change was on the way to becoming a reality.

The challenge of changing things means that some will change with you and some won't. In fact, if you have ever seen the bell curve, you will understand what I am talking about. When dealing with change, there are usually a few—about 3 percent—who are quick to change with you. These are your early adaptors. They are usually enthusiasts, like myself, who thrive on change. These people are the ones you want to be sure to sit down with and let them know where you are headed because they can bring others with them. The next group brings at least twice as many with them, and they are just behind the first group and will get on board with your idea when they see some of the early adaptors responding well. The majority of people are somewhere in the middle and will change after they understand the need for the change and have a few facts to back up the reason the change is needed. The curve then takes a downward turn and mirrors itself on the other half. There will be those who drag behind the majority, and unfortunately there will be another 3 percent or so who may never agree to the change. One of the main reasons to begin to communicate change early is because of these last few. The longer they have to process the change, the better off everyone is. The good thing about this group is that they can usually give you some good reasons not to change and will help you to see where the problem areas in the change might be. I like to take on this group early, one-on-one, and face-to-face. This communicates that you are listening to them. They may never agree, but your plan will be more fine-turned when you hear the pros and the cons.

Imagine that we are starting to change our women's programming because we have realized that some of the things we are doing may not be allowing us to focus on the main things of evangelism, discipleship, and ministry. Let's say that we have one DVD-driven women's Bible study on Tuesday mornings, and we see the need to add some other options that would train women how to study the Word for themselves. We need to add a study with possibly several teachers who would help women do this. We would begin by communicating the need for in-depth study and more training. We might offer a course on what the Bible says about what women's leadership should look like. We might tell about some things that are being successfully offered elsewhere. We must create the need for the change and help women to see it before we charge forward and offer the course. Instead of putting these two studies at the same time, we might think about offering one of the studies at night and even in a home setting. It might be possible to have some on Thursday morning or even Sunday afternoon. Brainstorming with several on our team will help to ease the process. It will be of the utmost importance to communicate with the facilitator of the existing study. Good communication is essential in change. It is also possible that we will have several offerings so as not to put the two in competition with each other. Once the change has been made, it will be important to celebrate the things that have happened—maybe more were reached for Christ, more women were prepared to teach Bible studies, more women were given the opportunities to come to the studies because of the time change. These principles that come out of John 2 can be applied in many settings.

As we implement the changes needed, it will require some tweaking. As I came on board at Southern Seminary, I saw the need for more options in our lay training Women's Ministry Institute. We had a great foundation, and we were ready to offer more courses. As we added these, it became apparent that we had added too many choices. Imagine that—too many choices for women. As soon as I realized what was happening, we enlisted a woman to call numbers of women in the Louisville area to find out just what their needs were. We also pulled together a group of women who were involved with our training at various levels—teachers, students, office assistants, those serving in the local church, and others—who gave needed input. We brainstormed all the options and then tested the ideas with others. When it was time to make the changes, we were able to send out a letter, and the women were excited about what was happening because they knew we had really listened to them and taken their input to heart. Making adjustments to ministry areas is a continual process. When we fail to make changes, we can sometimes come across as a stagnant pond. We don't change for the sake of change, but we continue to evaluate, and we change as needed. It is easy to celebrate with everyone because they know that they have been a part in making the ministry better.

Change when needed is good and beneficial. However, almost every change leads to some sort of conflict. We always pray that the conflict is minor, but conflict can happen at any moment. It too has been around since the beginning of time.

FROM THE BEGINNING, CONFLICT . . .

No matter how perfect the environment, there still can be conflict. As long as people have been on the earth, conflict has been around. Remember Adam's family? Cain and Abel had a huge conflict that resulted in Cain killing Abel. Conflict is a part of life, and effective leaders need to be able to deal with it. While there are numerous passages and people in the biblical account, there is one at which we need to take a closer look in an attempt to understand the biblical principles of how a leader handles conflict.

A BIBLICAL CASE STUDY ON CONFLICT

One of the most admired leaders in the Bible, right up there with Moses and Jesus, is Nehemiah. He was an incredible leader. While space will not allow me to point out every aspect of his leadership, it will enable me to focus on the way Nehemiah handled conflict. As the account began in Nehemiah 1, Nehemiah was in Susa where he was serving as the cupbearer to the king. Hanani, one of his brothers, and some other men came in. The story continues in verses 3 and 4 of Nehemiah 1,

> *They said to me, "The survivors in the province, who returned from the exile, are in great trouble and disgrace. Jerusalem's wall has been broken down, and its gates have been burned down." When I heard these words, I sat down and wept. I mourned for a number of days, fasting and praying before the God of heaven (Neh 1:3–4).*

CONSIDERED THE PROBLEM—NEHEMIAH 1:2–3

Nehemiah first considered the problem at hand. He heard the terrible news that his people had been in a great conflict. Nehemiah listened to the report and asked questions. It was important that he gain reliable information so that he could formulate his plan. He took time to mourn, fast, and pray for several days. This is how a good leader responds when in conflict. The leader analyzes the problem and looks at it from every possible angle. Being able to respond to the problem rather than reacting to it is always preferred. Listening and hearing are also important. Asking questions is the best way to make sure all the information is gathered. The fact that Nehemiah took time to mourn suggests that he had a handle on his emotions.

COMPASSIONATE HEART—NEHEMIAH 1:4

The next important truth we learn from this look at Nehemiah is that he had a compassionate heart. Throughout this book Nehemiah had a real concern for the people and what they were going through. He was concerned with their "great trouble and disgrace" (Neh 1:3). Nehemiah's heart was heavy for the Jewish people. In his prayer in Nehemiah 1:5–11, we sense his anguish and feel his compassionate heart.

CONSULTED GOD—NEHEMIAH 1:4–11

The prayer that Nehemiah prays is important because leaders are to pray specifically. The third aspect of Nehemiah's leadership is that he consulted God. He acknowledged that God is great and awesome and One who keeps His covenant with those He loves and who follow His commands. He asked for forgiveness for the Israelites, including himself and his family. He remembered that he and his people had not followed God's commands and had even acted wickedly toward Him. He prayed for success and for favor as he approached the king. Nehemiah modeled the importance of prayer and fasting (see verse 4). Prayer allows the leader to get God's perspective on the conflict at hand as well as His perspective on the involvement of the leader and the possible solutions to the problem.

CONTINUED TO WAIT—NEHEMIAH 2:1–10

Nehemiah waited patiently for God's perfect timing. He continued to wait. It was four months before he would see the opening that God gave him before the king. We can find the biblical account in chapter 2, verses 1–10. Because Nehemiah had prayed and planned, he was waiting on the time and door that God would open. When the opening came, Nehemiah was ready for it. Even though there had been months to prepare, he still breathed a prayer to the Lord just before he spoke. Leaders must be willing to wait on the timing before they jump into a situation, especially one with the magnitude that this carried. While some leaders avoid conflict and others run toward it, Nehemiah found God's balance. Timing can be a major factor in resolving conflict.

CALCULATED THE SITUATION—NEHEMIAH 2:11–16

As Nehemiah arrived on the scene in Jerusalem, he did so in quiet. He examined the scene. Nehemiah did not blow the trumpets or stage a parade; he went there, stayed a few days, surveyed the area at night with only a few men, and examined the walls and the gates that had been destroyed. He did not even reveal to anyone his plan to save the day. He could have revealed his strategy when he arrived but waited and checked everything out first. Investigating the full extent of the problem is crucial in leadership.

CALLED THE TEAM—NEHEMIAH 2:17–20

After this Nehemiah called his team together. They would be an essential part of the reconciliation project, and it was important to inform them of what would happen and how. We can read his words to them in verses 17–20 in chapter 2. He carefully draws them in by reminding them of the trouble and disgrace and quickly challenging them to build the wall together with his support. He brings their focus back to God and His support before anyone has a chance to say no. He shares the story of being before the king and being granted favor. The troops reply with a "let us start rebuilding," and the work begins. Even in the face of mocking and ridicule (more conflict), He reminds the group against them of the One who is in charge. The job of a leader is never finished. After all the pressure and waiting, Nehemiah could have backed down and said he had been wrong to try such a huge task as rebuilding the wall; however, he continued to work the plan and stayed right on course. Strong leaders continue to evaluate and reevaluate but do not back out because of a little mocking and ridicule.

CONTINUED CONSTRUCTION—NEHEMIAH 2:17–20

While the wall reconstruction had just begun, the construction continued. By reading the rest of Nehemiah, we can gather valuable truths about leadership. In the following chapters Nehemiah enlists people to build the section of the wall where they lived. Continued building and construction requires ownership. People must own the plan and make it theirs. When the people knew the wall by them would be their protection, they had to have been more concerned with how they were building it. Nehemiah continues to deal with conflict after conflict, but he still follows these simple steps for dealing with it.

CONFLICT IS INEVITABLE

Handling conflict is something that every leader needs to be able to do. Regardless of the individual, he or she can always learn to be more effective. No matter what method or set of rules or stages is used, God is always there with much more insight to the problem than the leader has and stands ready to give insight and His presence in the midst of difficult situations.

All kinds of conflict can happen in any given group. I know of a real situation where some women got so frustrated with their pastor and the church because they were not reaching people as these ladies thought they should. They got so mad that they went and started their own church! They wonder why they are not funded as a church start. This is not the way to handle conflict. I know of another place where a lady wanted to host an event. When the pastor did not agree to let her have it, she got mad, took a bunch of women with her, and went to another church that would host her event. There is also the lady who, even though the women's ministry leader told her she could not have a Valentine's banquet, got up to make an announcement at an event, told the whole story, and proclaimed she was hosting it anyway. No wonder there is conflict in the church.

The conflict that I hear the most about that crosses even denominational lines is the conflict of different women's groups in the church. This is a sad thing when women cannot serve the local church together. More often that not, I hear the story of one group organization that has been around a long time and others that are new or forming. It stands to reason that there is the potential for conflict so this is one of the reasons that communication is necessary. Too often I hear the stories of a missions group and a women's ministry group that cannot seem to come together, and this can be a difficult thing and a source of conflict.

Let's look at how we might take care of a conflict between the established group of women in the church and a new group that is starting. First, we consider the problem. The two leaders should get together and hear each other out. Where exactly is the conflict? Are the groups ministering to the same people? What is the purpose of each? While each situation is different, it can often be a generation preference that is causing the conflict. It can also be a misunderstanding of the intentions of each group. A compassionate heart on the part of the leaders is also essential. It is usually the new group that must go to the established group to communicate. Hearts must be shared. The obvious place to start is that the two should consult God together. Praying together can bring great love and affection. It clears the air and allows women to see the needs and motives of the other. Continue to wait for God's timing. God knows the situation, and He will bring things to light as needed. Calculate the situation. Look at every angle. Then pull the team or teams, as the case may be, together. Weigh it all out, pray about it, and move on with the construction plan. What needs to happen? Get the input of the team and wise counsel, make a decision, and move forward. It is not that we mow over or avoid anyone; it is that we move to a conclusion to the conflict. Resolutions do not always mean that everyone agrees with the decision. Resolutions mean that we put the conflict to rest, and we do not continue to dwell on it. Ultimately, it is best to work together, but to choose to work separately can sometimes be a resolution, though not a good one. I learned years ago that we can make all of the people happy some of the time, make some of the people happy all the time, but we cannot make all of the people happy all the time. Welcome to leadership and conflict resolution.

CONFLICTS WITH INDIVIDUALS

We looked at Nehemiah and how he dealt with team changes and conflict, but it is important to mention that often even in the church there will be conflicts between two women. As we deal with these, we start with Matthew 18 as our principle:

> *If your brother sins against you, go and rebuke him in private. If he listens to you, you have won your brother. But if he won't listen, take one or two more with you, so that by the testimony of two or three witnesses every fact may be established. If he pays no attention to them, tell the church. But if he doesn't pay attention even to the church, let him be like an unbeliever and a tax collector to you. I assure you: Whatever you bind on earth will have been bound in heaven, and whatever you loose on earth is already loosed in heaven. Again, I assure you: If two of you on earth agree about any matter that you pray for, it will be done for you by My Father in heaven. For where two or three are gathered together in My name, I am there among them (Matt 18:15–20).*

Just as the Scripture says, we go to the person with whom we have a conflict. When a woman comes to us to complain about a sister in Christ, we are to encourage that woman to go to the sister and talk to her. God set this command in place to protect us. We can be easily entangled in "cross-talk" when we do not follow this principle. I define *cross-talk* as the talk behind the scenes where the two accuse each other and us of all sorts of things to "prove their case" against the other. As soon as we approach the sister against whom the complaint is lodged, we set ourselves up for some complicated messes. Encourage the women who have a problem to talk to the other sister—even when it is a teacher or one of the leaders, even when it is the pastor or another staff member. There are always two sides to the problem so staying out of it is a wise thing to do. If the woman has gone to the sister and has not gotten through regarding her point, she is to take another with her. We should not assume that we should be the other person. We are not there to rescue anyone from all the misunderstandings that can happen. While there are libraries full of books on this subject, we are just touching on the main principle of helping the woman to follow the Word of God. If this sister happens to be one of the leaders of the ministry, then there are times when we will need to be involved. The principle is that after the woman goes to the sister and is not heard, she is to take another with her. If that doesn't resolve the problem, then the Scripture says to take it to the church. As leaders of the ministry to women, this is where we might have to get involved. I have found it helpful, when it is necessary to meet, to pull everyone in to talk at the same time to avoid the "but she told me" syndrome that can easily happen. I do not consider myself a trained counselor, but I can follow the simple guidelines in handling conflict. In my experience women seldom ever go to the person to complain so it has been the rare occasion that I have had to get involved.

In Conclusion

Change and conflict can both be things that grow us and grow the women's leadership team. Neither are things about which we need to be overly concerned. Both are sometimes needed. After it is all over, hopefully we have grown and know that somehow we have honored God in the way we handled everything.

Questions for Discussion

On Change

1. What are some of the changes that took place in the early church found in the book of Acts? Select one of the chapters or stories and discuss how you might handle each situation.
2. Write some case studies on change. These can be real situations that happened. Get in groups and discuss how you would apply the principles from the Bible in each case.

ON CONFLICT

1. Read through Acts again and look for the conflicts. Discuss some of your favorites and determine what the plan of action might be if you had the same or a similar situation.
2. Write some case studies on conflict. Discuss how, as a leader, you would handle each conflict.
3. Discuss some individual conflicts (without giving names) and how these conflicts were handled. What did you learn from each case?

Chapter 15

Women's Ministry with Excellence

Terri Stovall

*My eager expectation and hope is that I will not be
ashamed about anything, but that now as always,
with all boldness, Christ will be highly honored in my
body, whether by life or by death (Phil 1:20).*

At a women's ministry conference, a number of breakout sessions were geared around the various programs
that are included in a typical women's ministry. There
was a session on mentoring, women's Bible studies, special events,
retreats, missions, and such. By the time I was sitting in my third
breakout session, I noticed a common theme in the questions asked
during each session. The questions were asked in different ways,
but they all seemed to want to know who was doing "it" successfully and what were they doing. The women's ministry leaders were
honestly seeking help to make their own ministries more successful. Later that weekend, on Sunday morning, I had the television

on while getting ready for church. I started flipping through the various church services currently being aired. Over and over again I saw sermon series titles such as *How to Have a Successful . . . Marriage . . . Life . . . Job . . .* you fill in the blank. Success seems to be something that many people desire.

Success can be defined and measured in so many different ways. But in ministries how is success defined? Success can be measured by numbers, programs, size, tenure, accolades, or a host of other variables, but this may not be the same way that God measures success. God expects women's ministry to excel at His word, His truth, His plan, and His call. It sounds like a tough standard, but it is God's standard. God gives leaders in women's ministry a vision of what He wants us to be and do. Sometimes in the midst of doing ministry, we lose sight of success in God's eyes. Oswald Chambers writes of Paul and his vision, "Paul was devoted to a Person not to a cause. He was absolutely Jesus Christ's, he saw nothing else, he lived for nothing else."[1] This brings us back to the question at hand. What are the characteristics of a successful women's ministry and ministry leader of excellence?

Characteristics of Excellence

A number of characteristics can describe a women's ministry of excellence. We have narrowed those down to 10.

Keeps Christ and the Bible Central

A successful women's ministry keeps Christ and the Bible central. Paul wrote in his letter to the Corinthian church, "For I determined to know nothing among you except Jesus Christ and Him crucified" (1 Cor 2:2). Christ is the central force and focus of all we do. His sacrifice on the cross, His resurrection, and the life He promises are our mission. The Bible—the inerrant, infallible Word of God—is our map, curriculum, and message

---

[1] O. Chambers, "January 24," *My Utmost for His Highest* (Oswald Chambers Publications, 1963).

from God. It is all sufficient, God breathed, alive, and active and cuts to the core of our soul like nothing else on this earth. To drift toward programs, studies, personalities, or standards that detract from Christ or the Bible takes us off course from Jesus' command for our lives. Many may say that Christ is pre-eminent in their ministry and the Bible is central to all they do, but upon closer examination the reality shows a sidelined view of Scripture and a cursory nod to Christ. Start here with this first characteristic, and the rest will fall in place. Keep Christ and His Word central in all you do.

UNDERSTANDS AND CELEBRATES BIBLICAL WOMANHOOD

A women's ministry of excellence understands and celebrates biblical womanhood. Because of today's cultural pull to be politically correct and tolerant, this can be one of the more difficult yet rewarding distinctives to maintain. Notice that the starting point is to understand biblical womanhood. When the women's ministry leader fully grasps the gift God has given women through His design for manhood and womanhood, then she can live it, model it, teach it, and celebrate it with the women in her church. For many women the freedom they experience when they begin to live as they were created to be is almost overwhelming. The struggles women face today can often be quieted as they embrace that we are all created equal, that men and women have unique roles to fill, and it is OK that the roles are not the same. In fact, when they finally embrace true biblical womanhood, many feel that they have found their place and purpose in life. What a gift a women's ministry can give to the women they are reaching by understanding and celebrating biblical womanhood.

LED BY AND FOR WOMEN

A women's ministry of excellence is best led by women and is specifically for women. This does not mean that a successful women's ministry must have a women's ministry leader as

part of the paid church staff. Rather, this means that a successful women's ministry should be woman-to-woman ministry. A
male staff member may supervise a volunteer leader or even a
paid leader, but women minister best to women. When I left my
position as minister to women to join the faculty at Southwestern, the church gave the women's ministry to the minister of
discipleship, a male. This man of God struggled with how best
to run a women's ministry. I received several phone calls from
him in which I tried to help him understand the ministry, understand the women, and understand that, as wonderful as he was,
the ladies really needed a female to whom they could relate. It
was not long before the pastor's administrative assistant became
the unofficial staff liaison with the women's ministry. Women
are the best leaders for ministry to women.

A women's ministry of excellence is not only led by women
but should also be for women, not men and women. The growth
of Bible studies for women seems to have outpaced Bible studies targeted specifically to men. Therefore, a growing number of
women's ministries have had requests for men to join the Bible
studies with the women. There is a time for couples and mixed
genders to gather for study together, but the women's ministry
is not that time. A number of women's ministries have had to
note specifically on their publicity materials that Bible studies
or special events are for women only. Do not apologize for that.
God knew what He was doing when He instructed the older
women to teach the younger women and the older men to teach
the younger men. This is an opportunity for women to be taught,
mentored, and challenged by another woman. Women's ministry
is for women.

Operates Under Authority

A women's ministry of excellence operates under the authority of the pastor and church leadership. This does not contradict
the previous distinctive that women's ministry should be led by
women. Rather, this serves as a reminder that women best lead

as they willingly place themselves under the authority of their pastor and church leaders. One of the things that I hear from pastors is that they have had problems with women's ministries in general and their leaders specifically. Further inquiry reveals it is because they do not listen to the direction of the pastor or they go off on their own tangent, doing a lot of good things that do not match the direction and mission of that church. This one area, more than any other, is why many pastors face women's ministries with fear and trepidation or, at the very least, a cautious optimism. Ladies, when Christ and the Bible are central to all she does and she understands biblical womanhood, a women's ministry leader cannot help but serve under the authority of those God has placed over her. If the pastor says, "I don't think that's what we need to do right now," do not take his decision as a personal attack on you or the women's ministry. God has placed that pastor as an overseer and leader for that church. God has given that pastor a vision for that local church. Our job is to do all we can to work with him in order to accomplish the mission and vision of the church. A successful women's ministry leader serves under the authority of the pastor and church leadership.

MODELS TITUS 2 MINISTRY

A women's ministry of excellence models a Titus 2 ministry. The overarching goal of a women's ministry is to make disciples. God outlined a plan and a curriculum to accomplish that goal in Titus 2. Making disciples is walking with women through life, teaching them how to be women of God, to be good wives to their husbands, to raise their children, to provide a nurturing home, and to navigate the rough waters of life. To model a Titus 2 ministry is more than offering a mentoring program. It is modeling a lifestyle where women come together as the family of God, encouraging, teaching, and helping one another. Starting with the leader, it is investing in the lives of women to help them become all that God intended for them to be. The women's ministry of excellence is characterized by a Titus 2 lifestyle.

REACHES WOMEN FOR CHRIST

A women's ministry of excellence does all it can do to reach as many women as possible for Christ. One only has to browse the bookstore shelves or watch women's talk shows and networks to realize that there has been an explosion in the hunt for the spiritual. Women who seemingly have it all are still searching for meaning, acceptance, and love. Women who have experienced debilitating loss wonder whether there is anything in which they can place their hope and trust. In between are women who are simply searching for peace, love, forgiveness, direction, and purpose.

Those of us who have experienced salvation in Christ know that He is the answer. One of the best ways for a woman to hear the gospel of Christ is when it is shared by another woman. In many cultures the only way a woman will hear is if another woman tells her. Women's ministries can do so much more than offer opportunities for the lost to come to the church. The most successful ministries train women to share their faith and to seek out opportunities to build relationships with those who need to know Christ. They intentionally go out for the purpose of sharing the hope that is available to a hopeless world.

In his letter to the Romans, Paul wrote, "For it is written: As I live, says the Lord, every knee will bow to Me, and every tongue will give praise to God. So then, each of us will give an account of himself to God" (Rom 14:11–12). Note that *every* knee will bow and *every* tongue will give praise, not just those who have professed Christ. There will come a day when all will realize that Jesus is the Messiah, but for some it will be too late. This should be a time of looking around and celebrating a family reunion rather than regretting that the message was never shared with a neighbor, a relative, a coworker, or a friend. May it not be a time when we give an account to God as to why we didn't tell another about the gift of life found in Jesus. Successful women's ministries do all they can to reach as many women as possible for Christ.

NURTURES WOMEN IN THEIR FAITH

A women's ministry of excellence nurtures women in their faith. Remember, the Great Commission gives two steps to making disciples. The first is to reach them for Christ. The second is to teach them His commands. A successful women's ministry cannot stop with evangelism but also disciples or nurtures women in their faith. Nurturing is more than offering or participating in Bible studies and mentoring programs. It is walking with women to growth and maturity. It is watching them grow into disciple makers themselves. A recent study found that those who actively share their faith, intentionally build relationships with the lost, and lead people to Christ are the mature believers.[2] Typically it is believed that adults who accept Christ win more people to Christ because they have more relationships with the lost. This is true in the short run. But the mature believer who has become a disciple maker herself is the true evangelist. Her motivation in life is to make disciples. She is the one who does not simply target those whom she already knows but intentionally seeks out those who need Christ. A successful women's ministry nurtures women to the point of becoming disciple makers themselves.

INVOLVES WOMEN IN KINGDOM WORK

A women's ministry of excellence involves women in kingdom work. Part of the growth process of a believer is finding a place to serve. Here again intentionality is the key. Many women want to serve, but they do not know where the best place is or even how to start to find that place. A women's ministry can help a woman find the right fit for her. God gives each believer

---

[2] G. L. Hawkins and C. Parkinson, *Reveal: Where Are You?* (Chicago: Willow Creek, 2007), 33.

spiritual gifts to be used for the body. Every woman has skills and areas of interest that tug at her. All women have life experiences and have moved through various life stages. A women's ministry can help a woman match the gifts she has been given with the skills, interests, and life experiences to find just the right fit in service for her. That means that a women's ministry should know what opportunities of service are available and serve as a connection point between women and various ministries. For women who have felt that they have nothing to offer, the experience of finding a place where God uses them in the lives of others can be a life-transforming experience in and of itself. A successful women's ministry involves, connects, and encourages women in kingdom work.

ENGAGES THE NEXT GENERATION

A women's ministry of excellence engages the next generation. A practical application of the Titus 2 lifestyle, the older engaging the younger, is true woman-to-woman ministry. Today five adult generations are in the church. The family today is separated by physical distance, divorce, busyness, and misplaced priorities. Each generation of women longs for connection with and guidance from those who are older. On a given Sunday morning, multigenerational families can be at the same church at the same time and never see one another until they meet for lunch. Teenage girls are searching for answers to love and relationships; young mothers want to know if they will ever sleep again; mothers of teens are looking for mentors to guide them through this tumultuous time; empty nesters are looking to rekindle marriages and explore new avenues of service, and so on. Each generation seeks guidance and insight from the generation before. Each generation can also give guidance and insight to the generation after. While it is difficult to program this ministry, a successful women's ministry provides avenues and opportunities to allow various ages to intersect, intentionally engaging the next generation.

SUPPORTS THE CHURCH AND ITS MINISTRIES

A women's ministry of excellence supports the church and its ministries. A women's ministry is not an isolated ministry that never involves itself in other areas of the church. A successful women's ministry can intentionally partner with other ministries to work together. The women's ministry leader will endear herself to the church and its leaders if she is the first to ask, "How can we help you?" A preschool and children's ministry leader who works as much with mothers as she does with the children will be your debtor when you come alongside her and offer assistance. A student minister will welcome the opportunity to have women who can work with the girls in his ministry. Whatever the ministry, a successful women's ministry sees itself as a part of a team, working together to accomplish the mission that God has given.

A WORD TO PASTORS AND CHURCH LEADERS

The vast majority of this text has been directed to the women's ministry leader, but women's ministry will have little success without the help and support of the pastors and church leaders. A women's ministry leader who is leading as God designed needs your leadership and direction. There are several ways that you can help your women's ministry and thereby help your church.

PRAY FOR THEM AND WITH THEM

A pastor can pray for and with the women's ministry and its leaders. You are their pastor and spiritual leader. If your women's ministry leader is new to this level of leadership, she is facing the daunting task of vision casting, decision making, developing leaders, standing on truth, dealing with criticism, and trying to maintain her own spiritual growth. Pray for her. The women's ministry can be one of the church's best tools for reaching women for Christ, but it too faces opposition and obstacles. Pray for those involved with this ministry. Because of your position and your authority, the simple act of stopping by a leadership team meeting and asking to pray with team members can strengthen the sense of purpose in the women's ministry. The power is not in the praying but in the communication and connection with God. If you do nothing else for the women in this ministry, pray for them and with them.

ENCOURAGE THEM

A pastor can encourage the women's ministry and its leaders. God—in His wisdom, creativity, and maybe a little humor—has made women a little different from men. Even in a professional setting, women really want connection. That is why they communicate in so much detail. Men tend to be more bottom-line and get right to the point. Recognize that the women in your church need encouragement. I have learned that when I send an e-mail to a gentleman, I am best to get right to the point; the shorter the e-mail, the better. If I e-mail a woman, it is often perceived as being abrupt if I do not ask how she is doing or inquire about her family or ministry. Pastor, please encourage your women in all that they are doing. This does not have to be much. It can be anything from stopping a Bible study leader in the hall to thank her for what she is doing to a public accolade from the pulpit. Encourage the women's ministry through successes, difficulties, and challenges. Encourage them to stand firm on truth. Encouragement is like cool water to a woman's thirsty soul.

TEACH THEM

A pastor can teach the women's ministry, especially its leaders. As the pastor, you are the primary teacher for the church. You may not formally teach the women's ministry leaders, but there are many teachable moments in ministry. Holding the women's ministry accountable to remain centered on Christ and the Bible is teaching. Gentle correction when a leader may start to step out from under authority can be teaching. Giving advice and direction to a leader trying to make a decision can be teaching. Do not be afraid of the women's ministry and its leaders. You may be thinking, *I'm not afraid,* but many pastors face the women's ministry and its leaders with a bit of uneasiness. You are their pastor, their authority, and their teacher. Teach them to observe all that God has commanded.

PARTNER WITH THEM

A pastor can partner with a women's ministry. The women of the church, especially the mature women and leaders, can be a wonderful resource for you in ministry. Partner with them to help with hospital visitation. A woman in the hospital can often be more open about her fears and concerns with another woman than she can with her male pastor. What a reservoir to pull from if you know there are women to whom you can turn when another woman in your church is facing a personal crisis. Probably half of your church consists of adult women. You are still their pastor, but use your women to help you minister to the vast needs that women face today. When you partner with them in ministry, there will be opportunities to see women and families come to faith in Christ. When the women's ministry has been taught by you to model biblical womanhood and to teach that to others, families will be strengthened. Pastors who partner with their women's ministries and leaders find new avenues to make a difference in the lives of people.

CONCLUSION

The purpose of this chapter is to bring together the key elements of the entire text. Women's ministry and women in leadership have tremendous influence on churches and ministries today. So many times it is not what a women's ministry does that causes problems but how it is done. A discipleship course that never considers Scripture is a problem. A leader who decides to go against a pastor's decision is a problem. A popular women's Bible study that has 50 women attend every week but who never share the gospel with the woman next door is a problem. A plethora of good programs and conferences are available that can give you some how-tos for ministry. These pages did not take that approach. It is not so much knowing the steps to take or the programs to use but understanding the biblical precepts through which everything flows. As you, a woman in leadership, remain committed to Christ, the Word of God, and His truth, you will know what to do. And if you ever get stuck, just ask Him for help. He will give you guidance along the way. Women are reaching women for Christ. Women are investing in the lives of women, nurturing them in their faith, and helping them find a place of service. Women are engaging the next generation of girls. And women are serving the church and the body of Christ. Women leading women—that is the biblical model for the church.

We have answered the questions of why, who, what, and how women lead women. Where you take it depends on you.

Suggested Resources for Women Leading Women

BIBLICAL FOUNDATION

Beck, J. R., and C. Blomberg, eds. *Two Views on Women in Ministry*. Grand Rapids: Zondervan, 2001.

Clouse, B., and G. Clouse, eds. *Women in Ministry: Four Views*. Downers Grove, IL: InterVarsity, 1989.

Hove, R. *Equality in Christ*. Wheaton, IL: Crossway, 1999.

Kassian, M. *The Feminist Mistake: The Radical Impact of Feminism on Church and Culture*. Westchester: Crossway, 2005.

Kassian, M. *Women, Creation and the Fall*. Westchester, IL: Crossway, 1990.

Maynard, M. H. *We're Here for the Churches*. Nashville: LifeWay, 2001.

Patterson, D. K., and R. H. Kelley, eds. *Women's Evangelical Commentary: New Testament*. Nashville: B&H, 2006.

_____, eds. *The Women's Study Bible*. Nashville: Thomas Nelson, 1995.

Piper, J., and W. Grudem, eds. *Recovering Biblical Manhood and Womanhood: A Response to Evangelical Feminism*. Westchester, IL: Crossway, 2006.

Strauch, A. *Men and Women, Equal yet Different: A Brief Study of the Biblical Passages on Gender*. Littleton, CO: Lewis and Roth, 1999.

LEADERSHIP PRINCIPLES

Adams, C., ed. *Transformed Lives: Taking Your Women's Enrichment Ministry to the Next Level*. Nashville: LifeWay, 2000.

_____, ed. *Women Reaching Women: Beginning and Building a Growing Women's Ministry*. Nashville: LifeWay, 2005.

Biehl, B. *Leading with Confidence*. Lake Mary, FL: Aylen, 2005.

Blackaby, R., and H. Blackaby. *Spiritual Leadership*. Nashville: B&H, 2001.

Booher, D. *Your Signature Work: Creating Excellence and Influencing Others at Work*. Wheaton, IL: Tyndale House, 2004.

Collins, J. *Good to Great*. New York: Harper & Row, 2001.

Edwards, S., and K. Mathews. *New Doors in Ministry to Women: A Fresh Model for Transforming Your Church, Campus, or Mission Field*. Grand Rapids: Kregel, 2002.

Jaynes, S. *Building an Effective Women's Ministry*. Eugene, OR: Harvest House, 2005.

Kouzes, J., and B. Possner. *The Leadership Challenge*. San Francisco: Jossey-Bass, 1995.

Kraft, V., and G. Johnson. *Women Mentoring Women: Ways to Start, Maintain, and Expand a Biblical Women's Ministry*. Chicago: Moody, 2003.

Ligon, D. J., and S. Hunt. *Women's Ministry in the Local Church*. Wheaton, IL: Crossway, 2006.

Mabery-Foster, L. *Women and the Church: Reaching, Teaching, and Developing Women for Christ*. Nashville: Word, 1999.

New International Version. *The Leadership Bible*. Grand Rapids: Zondervan, 1998.

Saucey, R., and J. TenElshof. *Women and Men in Ministry: A Complementary Perspective*. Chicago: Moody, 2001.

Sumner, S. *Men and Women in the Church: Building Consensus on Christian Leadership*. Downers Grove, IL: InterVarsity, 2003.

Zenger, J. H., and J. Folkman. *The Extraordinary Leader: Turning Good Managers into Great Leaders*. New York: McGraw-Hill, 2002.

Zigarmi, D., K. Blanchard, M. O'Connor, and C. Edeburn. *The Leader Within: Learning Enough About Yourself to Lead Others*. Upper Saddle River, NJ: Prentice Hall, 2005.

THE TASKS OF WOMEN'S MINISTRY

Beougher, S., and M. Dorsett. *Women and Evangelism: An Evangelistic Lifestyle from a Woman's Perspective*. Wheaton, IL: Billy Graham Center, Institute of Evangelism, 1994.

Beougher, T., and A. Reid, eds. *Evangelism in a Changing World*. Eugene, OR: Wipf and Stock, 2002.

Bright, V., and B. Ball. *The Joy of Hospitality*. Orlando, FL: NewLife, 1996.

Coleman, R. E. *The Master's Way of Personal Evangelism*. Wheaton, IL: Crossway, 1997.

Courtney, V. *Your Girl: Raising a Godly Daughter in an Ungodly World*. Nashville: B&H, 2006.

Davis, J. L. *Girls' Ministry Handbook: Starting and Growing a Girls' Ministry in Your Church*. Nashville: LifeWay Church Resources, 2007.

Downs, T. *Finding Common Ground: How to Communicate with Those Outside the Christian Community . . . While We Still Can*. Chicago: Moody, 1999.

Ford, L. *A Curriculum Design Manual for Theological Education*. Nashville: Broadman, 1991.

Foster, R. J. *Celebration of Discipline*. San Francisco: HarperCollins, 1998.

Hunt, S. *Spiritual Mothering: The Titus 2 Model for Women Mentoring Women*. Wheaton, IL: Crossway, 1993.

Lewis, C. S. *Mere Christianity*. New York: HarperCollins, 2003.

Martin, J. *HeartCall: Women Sharing God's Heart*. Alpharetta, GA: North American Mission Board, 1999.

McDowell, J., and B. Hostetler. *Right from Wrong: What You Need to Know to Help Youth Make Right Choices*. Dallas: Word, 1994.

McRaney, W., Jr. *The Art of Personal Evangelism*. Nashville: B&H, 2003.

Olson, G. *Teenage Girls: Exploring Issues Adolescent Girls Face and Strategies to Help Them*. Grand Rapids: Zondervan, 2006.

Pippert, R. M. *Out of the Saltshaker and into the World: Evangelism as a Way of Life*. Downers Grove, IL: InterVarsity, 1999.

Prosperi, W. *Girls Ministry 101: Ideas for Retreats, Small Groups, and Everyday Life with Teenage Girls*. Grand Rapids: Zondervan, 2006.

Reid, A. *Introduction to Evangelism*. Nashville: B&H, 1998.

Reid, A., and D. Wheeler. *Servanthood Evangelism Manual*. Alpharetta, GA: North American Mission Board, 2000.

WOMEN'S MINISTRY IN PRAXIS

Barthel, T. K., and J. Dabler. *Peace Making Women: Biblical Hope for Resolving Conflict*. Grand Rapids: Baker, 2005.

Biehl, B. *Masterplanning*. Nashville: B&H, 1997.

Bonem, M., and R. Patterson. *Leading from the Second Chair: Serving Your Church, Fulfilling Your Role, and Realizing Your Dreams*. San Francisco: Jossey-Bass, 2005.

Bridges, William. *Managing Transitions: Making the Most of Change*. Reading, MA: Addison-Wesley, 1991.

Bryson, J. M. *Strategic Planning for Public and Nonprofit Organizations*. San Francisco: Jossey-Bass, 1995.

Buzzell, S., K. Boas, and B. Perkins, eds. *The Leadership Bible*. Grand Rapids: Zondervan, 2000.

Essentials for Excellence. Nashville: Lifeway Church Resources, 2003.

Furlong, Gary. *Conflict Resolution Toolbox: Models and Maps for Analyzing, Diagnosing, and Resolving Conflict*. San Francisco: Jossey-Bass, 2005.

Hemphill, K., and B. Taylor. *Ten Best Practices to Make Your Sunday School Work*. Nashville: Lifeway Church Resources, 2001.

Herrington, J., M. Bonem, and J. H. Furr. *Leading Congregational Change*. San Francisco: Jossey-Bass, 2000.

Hersey, P., K. H. Blanchard, and D. E. Johnson. *Management of Organizational Behavior: Leading Human Resources*. 8th ed. Upper Saddle River, NJ: Prentice Hall, Inc., 2001.

Kotter, J. P. *Leading Change*. Boston: Harvard Business School Press, 1996.

Malphurs, A. *Advanced Strategic Planning: A New Model for Church and Ministry Leaders*. Boston: Baker, 2005.

Rainer, T. S., and E. Geiger. *Simple Church: Returning to God's Process for Making Disciples*. Nashville: B&H, 2006.

Sweet, Leonard. *AquaChurch*. Loveland, CO: Group, 1999.

Scripture Index

Genesis

1	51
1:1–5	207
1:27	3, 5
1:27–31	51
1:31	3
2–4	51
2:7	5
2:15–25	51
2:18	18
2:18–20	5
2:22	5
2:23	18
3:16	18
38	7

Exodus

2:1–10	6
12	174
15:20–21	6

Numbers

23:19	70

Deuteronomy

6:5–9	144
20:2–4	143

Joshua

1:3–5	67
1:3–6	67
1:3–9	67
1:7–8	67
1:9	67
2	7

6	7
6:1–27	175
24:15	61

Judges

4–5	6
5:9	47

2 Samuel

2:1–4	175
4:9–12	175
5:17–25	175
7:18–29	175
11–12	8

2 Kings

22:14	6

1 Chronicles

16:34	56

2 Chronicles

34:22	6

Ezra

8:36	109

Nehemiah

1	216
1:1–11	175
1:2–3	216
1:3	217
1:3–4	216
1:4	216
1:4–11	217
1:5–11	217
2	175

2:1–10	217
2:11–16	218
2:17–20	218
4:1–6	175

Psalms

40:5	173
78:5–7	152
86:15	55
119:89–90	57
145:17	54

Proverbs

14:15	176
15:22	176
16:3	176
16:9	176
16:33	176
20:18	176
21:5	176
31	xii, 71

Song of Songs

2:15	173

Isaiah

6:3	54
43:19	206

Jeremiah

29:11–13	66, 171

Micah

6:8	60

Matthew

5:8	68

5:16	33	21:2–3	10	**Romans**	
9:17	212	**John**		3:23	125
10:1–10	9	1:14	129	5:8	125
10:5–42	111	1:17	129	6:23	125
12:49–50	34	1:38–39	112	10:9–10	125
14:23	175	1:41	113	11:33–36	33
16:18	34	2	214	12	133, 204
18	221	2:1–11	207, 208	12:6–8	59
18:5–7	11	4	10	12:10	42
18:15–20	221	4:1–26	9	14:11–12	229
20:20–28	133	4:1–42	10	15:13	56
22:37–40	31, 36, 94	6:38	175	16:3	12
23:12	60	7:53–8:11	9	16:27	55
25:14–30	63	8:1–12	9	25:9–11	33
25:21	63	8:44	129		
25:29	63	13:34–35	42	**1 Corinthians**	
26:7	11	14:6	53, 99, 129	1:10–11	13
26:36–46	175	14:9	122	2:2	225
27:55	10, 157	14:17	129	3:1–3	120
28:16–20	116	15:5	34	3:6	130
28:18–20	31, 36, 93, 96,	17:17	129	3:6–9	34
	117, 150			5:16–21	133
Mark		**Acts**		11:2–16	12
3	189	1:8	110, 111	12	133, 204
3:13–15	189	1:13–14	11	12:4–7	131
7:26	10	2:4	34	12:12	188
10:45	114	2:42	41	12:12–17	34
12:42–43	10	2:46–47	157	12:12–26	160
14:3	11	4:31	100	12–14	40
15:40–41	10	5:14	12	12:25	42
16:14	117	5:42	111	12:28	60
		8:3	12	13	37
Luke		8:12	12	14:33	56
2:36	11	8:26–38	114	14:33–38	21
5:30–32	175	8:29	34	14:34	21
6:35–36	41	9:2	12	16:2	41
6:40	102	11:12	34	16:9	12
7:37	11	11:29	41		
8:1–3	10	13:4	34	**2 Corinthians**	
9:28	175	16:9–10	175	1:3–7	137
10:1–20	111	16:13	11	8:4	41
10:38–42	10	16:25–34	33		
11:1	175	17:4	12	**Galatians**	
12:11–12	103	17:12	12	1:10	71
13:16	9	17:27	106	3:28	20
14:28	186	22:4	12	4:3	42
15:32	108	26:9–18	114	5:22–23	58
19	114				

Ephesians

1:6	*33*
1:12	*33*
1:14	*33*
1:22–23	*34*
2:10	*132, 193, 213*
3:14	*34*
3:20–21	*xiv*
4	*204*
4:1–3	*69*
4:12	*69*
4:14	*69*
4:15–16	*34*
4:32	*42*
5:1	*40*
5:19	*41*
6:12	*177*

Philippians

1:9–11	*68*
1:20	*224*
2:1–11	*60*
2:1–18	*65*
2:3–4	*62*
3:10	*121*
3:12–14	*65*
4:2–3	*13*

Colossians

1:18	*34*
1:28	*40, 120, 122*
1:29	*121*

2:12–17	*92*
2:19	*34*
3	*40*
3:12	*58*
3:12–17	*82*
3:15–16	*40*
3:16	*41*
3:23–24	*77*

1 Thessalonians

5:11	*42, 74*

1 Timothy

1:5	*37*
1:18–19	*142*
2:1–2	*41*
2:8–11	*21*
2:11	*21*
2:12–15	*21*
4:13	*41*
5:1–2	*34*

2 Timothy

1:3–5	*13*
1:9	*132*
2:2	*104*
3	*100*
3:1–7	*100*
3:14–17	*103*
4:3–5	*1*
4:19	*12*

Titus

2	*ix, 228, 231*
2:1–5	*15*
2:3–5	*94, 143*

Hebrews

4:12	*129*
10:24	*42*
10:24–25	*29, 40*
13:15	*33*

James

4:10	*60*
5:16	*42*

1 Peter

1:17	*55*
2:9	*33*
4:10	*58, 105, 133*
4:10–11	*153*

2 Peter

3:9	*57*

1 John

3:14–18	*34*
3:17	*41*

3 John

1:8	*154*

Revelation

21:5	*207*

Consulting and Instructional Information

www.womenleadingwomen.com
(PowerPoint presentations can be accessed here.)

Authors' Contact Information

Jaye Martin
www.jayemartin.com/contact

Terri Stovall
P. O. Box 22367
Ft. Worth, TX 76122
817-923-1921, ext. 2159

tstovall@swbts.edu